M000250785

★Copyright © 1998 ONDORISHA PUBLISHERS., LTD. All rights reserved.
★Published by ONDORISHA PUBLISHERS.,LTD.
11-11 Nishigoken-cho, Shinjuku-ku, Tokyo 162-8708,Japan.
★ Sole Overseas Distributor: Japan Publications Trading CO., Ltd.
P. O. Box 5030 Tokyo International ,Tokyo, Japan.
★Distributed
· in United States by Kodansha America, INC.
114 Fifth Avenue, New York, NY 1011,U.S.A.
· in United Kingdom & Europe by Primier Book Marketing Ltd.,
1 Gower Street, London WC1E 6HA,England.
· in Australia by Bookwise International.
54 Crittenden Road, Findon, South Australia 5023, Australia.
10 9 8 7 6 5 4 3 2 1
ISBN4-88996-040-6

Full of flowers

Which flower do you like?   Let's have fun making bouquets.

instructions on page 32

instructions for framed picture of a flower on page 29.

wreath of
yellow flowers

tulip

rose

wreath of pink flowers

gerbera

potted plant

dandelion

horsetail

planters

Easy to make !

framed picture
of a flower(A)

framed picture
of a flower(B)

3

Animals in flocks

What charming eyes they have !! They are made of spangles.

instructions on page 35

Easy to make !

fish

cat(A)   cat(B)   cat(C)

cow   elephant   terrier   peacock

sheep   penguin   penguin   kangaroo   dachshund

pig   frog   cat(D)

tadpole   monkey   giraffe   ostrich

Home and garden

Let's make a town with colorful houses.

instructions on page 38

instructions for houses A,B on page 29

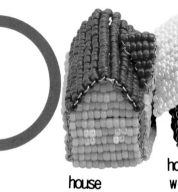

house
with red roof

house
with
yellow ro

house with orange roof

church

shop

shop

chair

church

flower cart

tree

arch

table

Easy to make !

house(B)

house(A)

7

Living room

You can make a doll house !!　All the furniture is made of beads.
It will be fun to change the furniture.

instructions on page 41

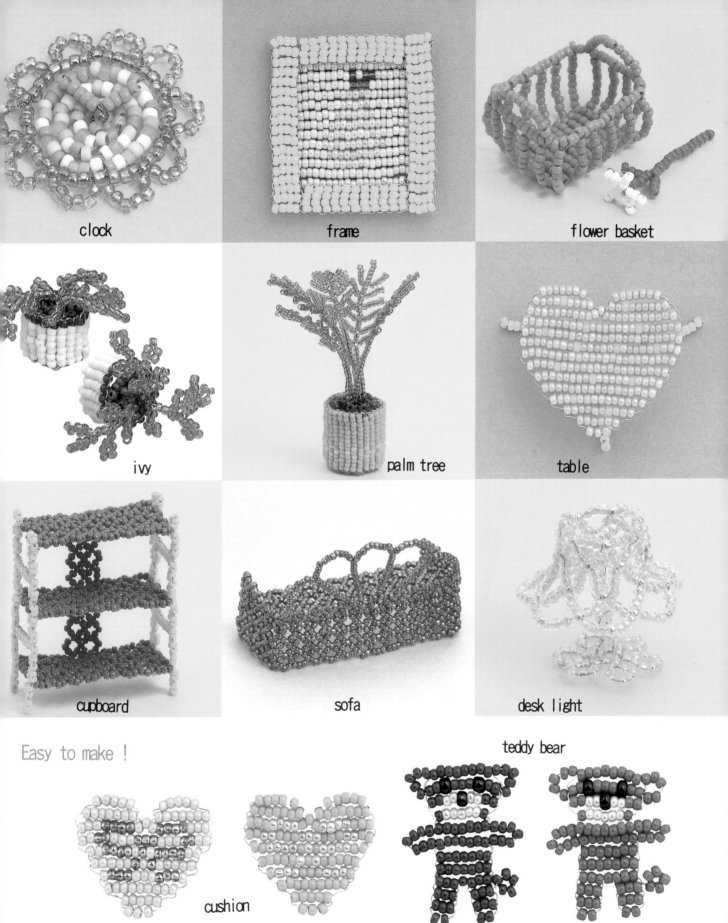

clock

frame

flower basket

ivy

palm tree

table

cupboard

sofa

desk light

Easy to make !

teddy bear

cushion

Afternoon on the street

You can make yourself comfortable,

putting these cute miniatures in your room.

instructions on page 44

instructions for mailbox on page 31

table

croissant

Swiss roll

candy

cheesecake

pastry

doughnut

jelly

chocolate cake

rice dumpling

pudding

fish-shape cake
(taiyaki)

Easy to make !

twist bread

French bread

15

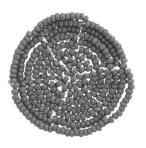

Plate(small size)

Restaurant

You can make dishes and foods individually.
Enjoy serving foods on your favorite plate.

instructions on page 51

deep-fried shrimp

16

onigiri(rice ball)

omelet

egg sunny-side up

plate(large size)

sushi

hamburg steak

salad bowl
(bottom view)

spaghetti

noodles

soup bowl
(bottom view)

lunch for children

salad

Easy to make !

chopsticks

spoon fork

knife

17

Kitchen ware

It's fun to put things into the miniatures you made.

instructions on page 54

instructions for basket on page 30

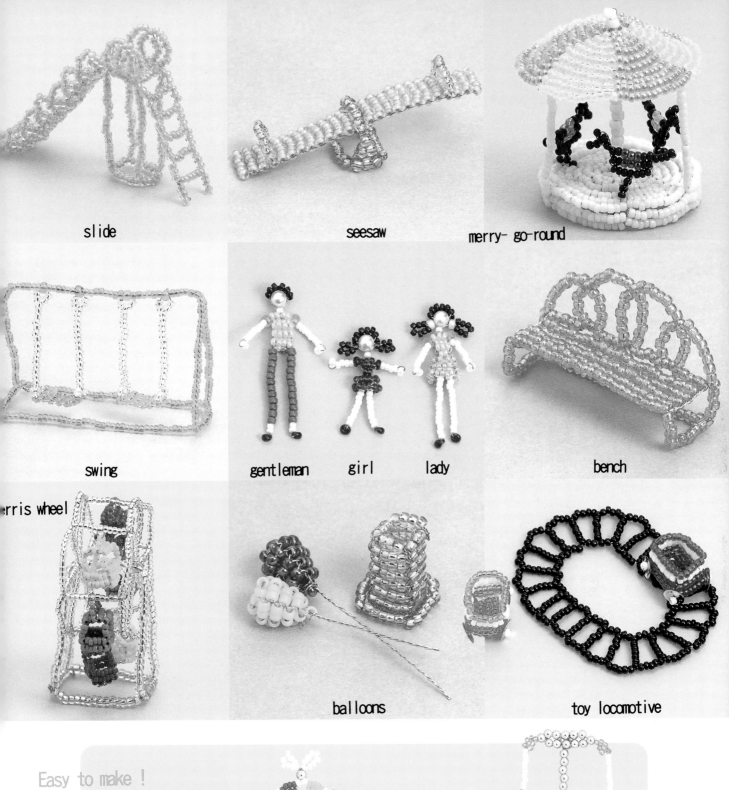

slide

seesaw

merry-go-round

swing

gentleman   girl   lady

bench

rris wheel

balloons

toy locomotive

Easy to make !

tea cup

parachute

23

Merry Christmas

When Christmas comes near, it will be nice to decorate
the Christmas tree with these angels, boots, candles, etc.
Put them on your bag as a good-luck charm.

instructions on page 62

socks

candy cane

angel

wreath

Santa Claus(A)

snowman

tree(A)

Santa Claus(A)

snowman

Yule Log

bell

candle

Easy to make !

star

Santa Claus(B)

tree(B)

25

About glass beads and useful tools

About glass beads

The miniatures in this book are made of the following beads.

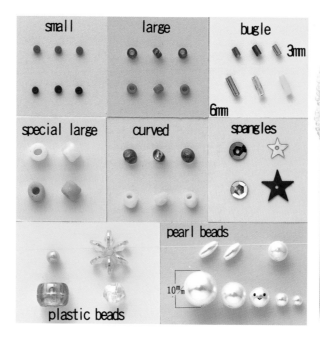

small

large

bugle

3mm

6mm

special large

curved

spangles

pearl beads

10mm

plastic beads

strung beads

loose beads
Collection of TOHO Craft

needle nose pliers

wire

craft glue

scissors

About useful tools

● The wire is sold at hobby shops in a small spool according to thickness, either 28, 30, 31, 34 gauge. There are three colors of wire, silver, gold and green to match the color of beads.
● needle nose pliers   Use to bend wires.
● scissors   Use to cut wires.
● craft glue   Glue is used to solidify the bead work.

How to string beads.

Pick up beads with the wire, moving beads with your finger tips. It's easy to handle beads which are spread over fabrics like felt on a lid or box.

How to string strung beads.

① First, let's make the side. After you make a flat rectangle, pass the wire left through the first line to make it into a pipe. Pass another end of the wire through the second line, then twist it and cut it.

upper part   wire 50cm

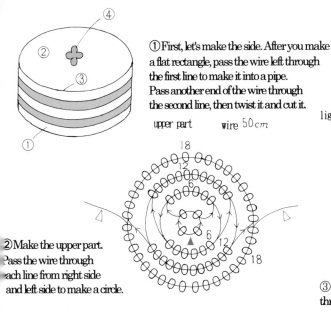

② Make the upper part. Pass the wire through each line from right side and left side to make a circle.

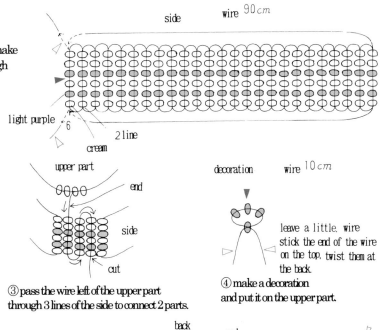

side   wire 90cm

light purple   6
2 line
cream

upper part

end
side
cut

③ pass the wire left of the upper part through 3 lines of the side to connect 2 parts.

decoration   wire 10cm

leave a little, wire stick the end of the wire on the top, twist them at the back.
④ make a decoration and put it on the upper part.

C Make 4 faces at a time.

Looking at the illustration, you may think it's so difficult, however, it's easy to work if only you follow the directions. In this case, you use more than two wires at a time, so be careful not to wind the wires.

back   red

wire ① 65cm
wire ② 65cm

8

side

silver   front   ⑨

• Page 10 •
Afternoon on the street

mailbox

Materials

mailbox: small round beads/red, silver
· wire#31/gold 130cm(42")

wire ①
00000000
wire ②

① pass 2 wires through 8 beads, they remain at the center of the wire.

2 line 00000000 ①
        00000000 ②

② make the second line with wire 1.

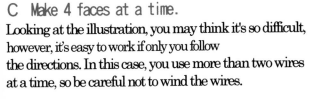

①   2 line
①② 1 line
②   2 line
②   3 line

③ make the third line with wire 2. ①②③ will be the upper part of the postbox.

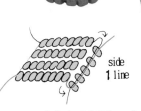

side
1 line

④ pass one end of wire 1 & 2 through 5 beads from right and left to make the first line of the side of the postbox.
⑤ make the first line of the other in the same way as ④.

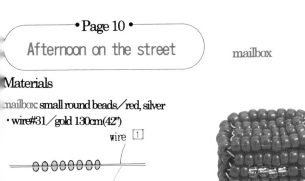

front 1 line

⑥ make the first line of the front and back of the postbox with the ends of wires of the side.

⑦ make both sides and the front and back in turns.
⑧ please notice the part where you make 3 lines of the side.
⑨ at the end, make 2 lines of the front and back, then pass the end of the wire through the side. Put them together, twist and bend them to the back. (refer to page 27 A)

31

Full of flowers potted plant✳planters

Materials

potted plant: small round beads／beige, green, blue, purple・wire#34／gold 210cm (84")・brown clay

planters: small round beads／green, yellow, salmon pink, orange・large round beads／beige・wire#34／・gold 350cm(140")・brown clay

▲=beginning △= ending

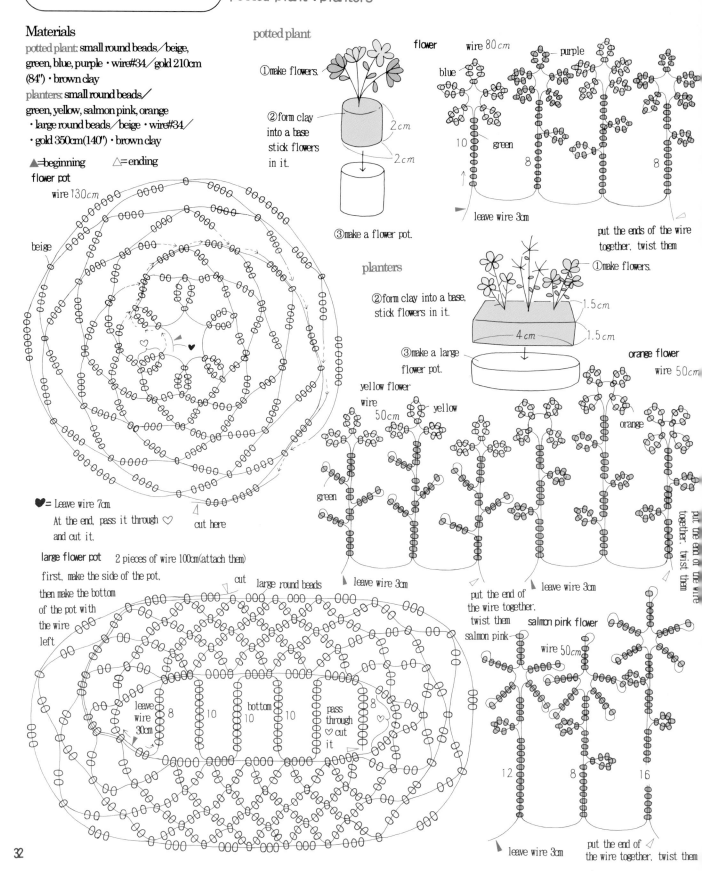

flower pot

wire 130cm

beige

potted plant

①make flowers.

②form clay into a base stick flowers in it.

2cm

2cm

③make a flower pot.

flower wire 80cm purple

blue

10 green 8 8

↑

▶ leave wire 3cm

put the ends of the wire together, twist them

♥= Leave wire 7cm
At the end, pass it through ♡ and cut it.

△
cut here

planters

②form clay into a base, stick flowers in it.

1.5cm

4cm

1.5cm

③make a large flower pot.

①make flowers.

orange flower
wire 50cm

yellow flower
wire 50cm yellow

orange

green

large flower pot 2 pieces of wire 100cm(attach them)
first, make the side of the pot, then make the bottom of the pot with the wire left

cut large round beads

leave wire 30cm 8 10 bottom 10 10 8 pass through ♡ cut it

▶ leave wire 3cm

put the end of the wire together, twist them

salmon pink flower
salmon pink

wire 50cm

▶ leave wire 3cm

put the end of the wire together, twist them

12 8 16

▶ leave wire 3cm

put the end of the wire together, twist them

put the end of the wire together, twist them

wreath of yellow flowers✳rose✳gerbera

Materials

wreath of yellow flowers: small round beads／clear green, muddy green, yellow, brown・wire#34／gold 110cm(44")

rose(for one <> different color. use same color of beads unless otherwise indicated): small round beads／beige<red>, yellow<pink>, yellow green・wire#34／gold 150cm(60")

gerbera(for one <> different color. use same color of beads unless otherwise indicated):small round beads／orange<pink> <yellow>, green, light pink<yellow><orange>, dark brown・wire#34／gold 100cm(40")

▲=beginning　　△=ending

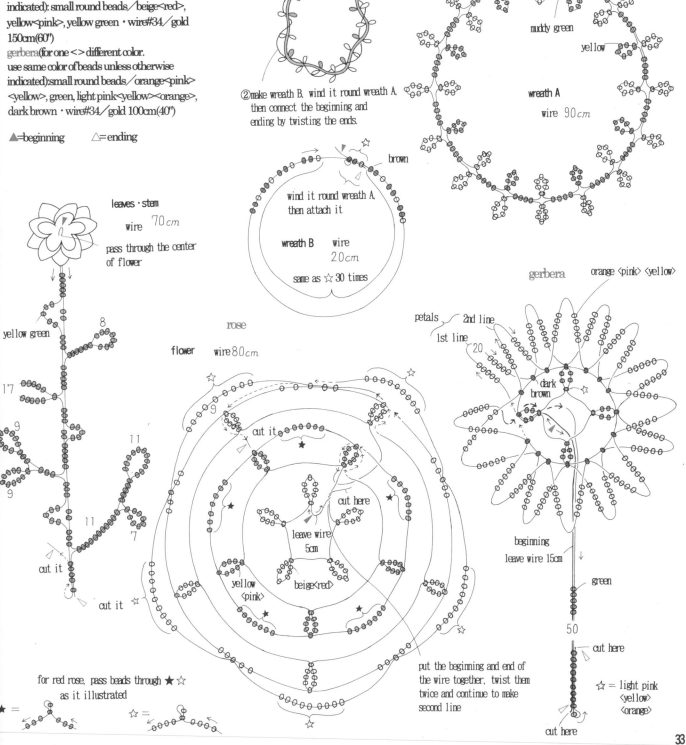

wreath of yellow flowers

①make wreath A. connect the end of beginning with ending by twisting them

②make wreath B. wind it round wreath A. then connect the beginning and ending by twisting the ends.

twist wires and attach them to the beginning

clear green

muddy green

yellow

wreath A
wire 90cm

brown

wind it round wreath A. then attach it

wreath B　wire 20cm

same as ☆ 30 times

leaves・stem
wire 70cm
pass through the center of flower

yellow green

8

17

9

9

11

11

7

cut it

cut it

rose
flower　wire 80cm

cut it

9

cut here

leave wire 5cm

yellow <pink>

beige<red>

put the beginning and end of the wire together, twist them twice and continue to make second line

for red rose, pass beads through ★ ☆ as it illustrated

★ =

☆ =

gerbera

orange <pink> <yellow>

petals　2nd line

1st line

20

dark brown

green

beginning
leave wire 15cm

50

cut here

☆ = light pink <yellow> <orange>

cut here

Full of flowers

wreath of pink flowers ✳ horsetail ✳ dandelion ✳ tulip

Materials

wreath of pink flowers: small round beads／
clear green, muddy green, pink, red・wire#34
／gold 130cm(52")

horsetail (for one): small round beads／
brown, white・wire#34／gold 50cm(20")

dandelion: small round beads／yellow, green
・wire#34／gold 180cm(72")

tulip(for one<>different color. use same
color of beads unless otherwise indicated):
small round beads／pink<red>, red<yellow>,
yellow green・wire#34／gold 260cm(104")

▲=beginning   △=ending

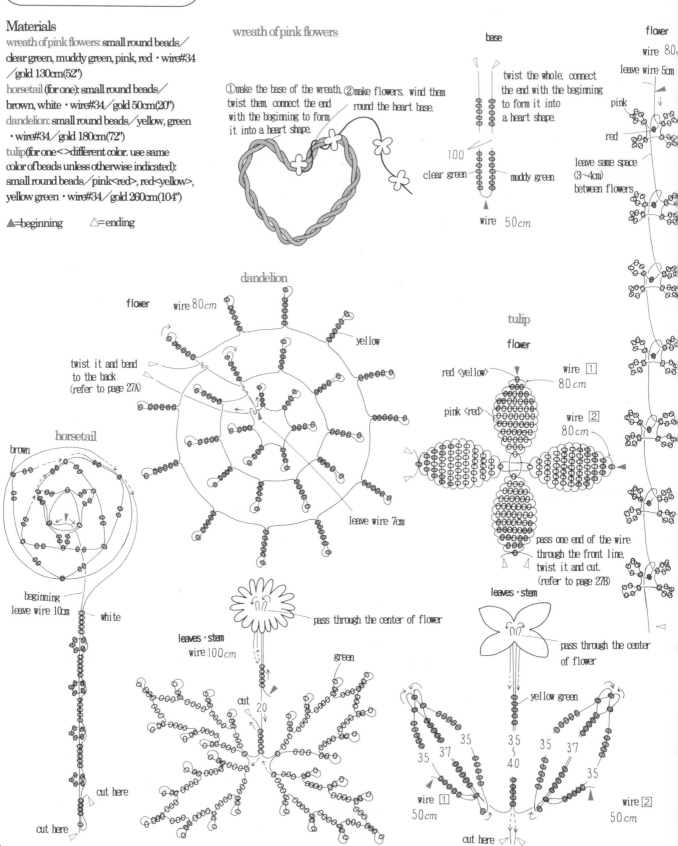

wreath of pink flowers

①make the base of the wreath. ②make flowers, wind them
twist them, connect the end   round the heart base.
with the beginning to form
it into a heart shape.

base

twist the whole, connect
the end with the beginning
to form it into
a heart shape.

100
clear green   muddy green

wire 50cm

flower
wire 80cm
leave wire 5cm
pink
red
leave same space
(3~4cm)
between flowers

dandelion

flower   wire 80cm
yellow
twist it and bend
to the back
(refer to page 27A)
leave wire 7cm

horsetail
brown
beginning
leave wire 10cm   white
cut here
cut here

leaves・stem
wire 100cm
cut
20
green
pass through the center of flower

tulip

flower
red <yellow>   wire ① 80cm
pink <red>   wire ② 80cm
pass one end of the wire
through the front line,
twist it and cut.
(refer to page 27B)

leaves・stem
pass through the center
of flower
yellow green
35   35   35   37   35
35   40
wire ①
50cm
wire ②
50cm
cut here

34

Materials

hexagon spangles 5mm white are used except for
cat A B C and monkey.

cat A: large round beads / white, gold, brown, black
· 4mm curved beads / red · wire #34 / silver
70cm(28")

cat B: small round beads / black, yellow · 3mm
curved beads / red · wire #34 / silver 50cm(20")

cat C: small round beads / white, orange, pink,
light blue · wire #34 / silver 50cm(20")

fish: small round beads / white, navy blue, black
· wire #34 / silver 30cm(12")

monkey: small round beads / brown, cream · large
round beads / brown, cream · 4mm special large /
cream · 8mm pearl beads / white · wire #34 /
silver 70cm(28")

sheep: small round beads / pink, violet, black
· large round beads / violet · wire #34 / silver
120cm(60")

giraffe: small round beads / yellow, brown, black
· large round beads / yellow, brown · wire #34 /
silver 130cm(52")

elephant: small round beads / gray, white, gold,
black · large round beads / gray · wire #34 /
silver 130cm(52")

cow: small round beads / white, black, beige
· large round beads / white, black, beige
· wire #34 / silver 120cm(48")

▲ = beginning   △ = ending

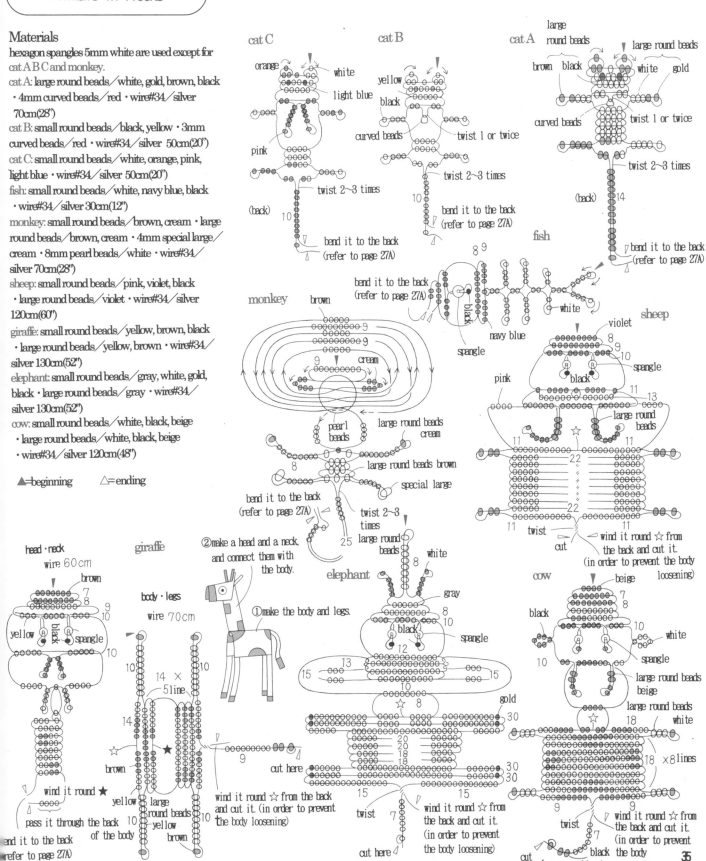

35

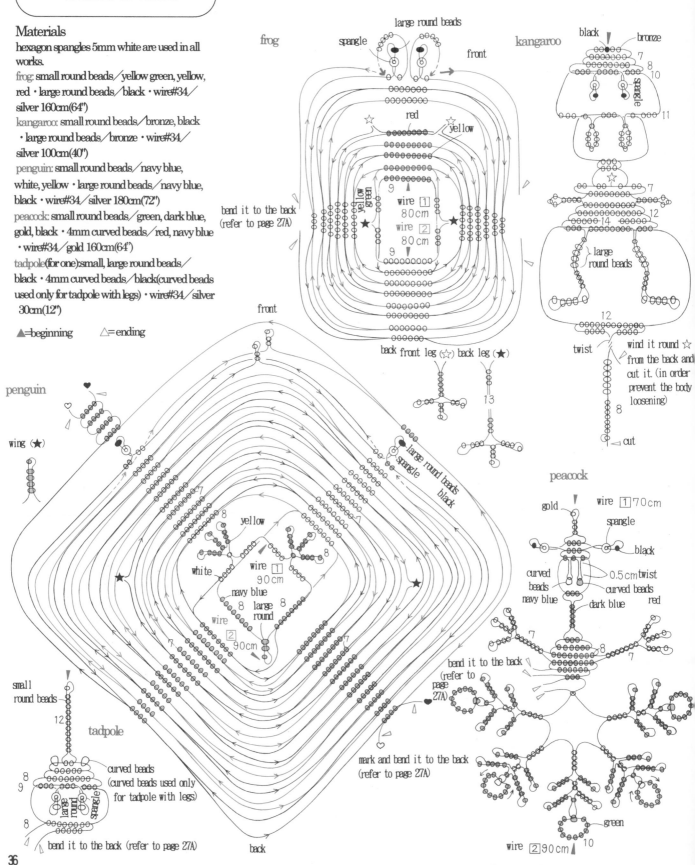

frog ✳ kangaroo ✳ penguin ✳ peacock ✳ tadpole

Materials

hexagon spangles 5mm white are used in all works.

frog: small round beads／yellow green, yellow, red・large round beads／black・wire#34／silver 160cm(64")

kangaroo: small round beads／bronze, black・large round beads／bronze・wire#34／silver 100cm(40")

penguin: small round beads／navy blue, white, yellow・large round beads／navy blue, black・wire#34／silver 180cm(72")

peacock: small round beads／green, dark blue, gold, black・4mm curved beads／red, navy blue・wire#34／gold 160cm(64")

tadpole(for one):small, large round beads／black・4mm curved beads／black(curved beads used only for tadpole with legs)・wire#34／silver 30cm(12")

▲=beginning   △=ending

frog

large round beads

spangle

front

red

yellow

9

yellow green

wire ①80cm

wire ②80cm

9

bend it to the back (refer to page 27A)

back front leg (☆) back leg (★)

13

kangaroo

black   bronze

7
8
10

spangle

11

large round beads

14   12

12

twist

wind it round ☆ from the back and cut it. (in order prevent the body loosening)

8

cut

penguin

♥
♡

wing (★)

front

large round beads spangle black

8

yellow

7

white

wire ①90cm

navy blue

8   large round

wire ②90cm

8

7

back

peacock

gold   wire ①70cm

spangle

black

curved beads navy blue

0.5cm twist

curved beads

dark blue

navy blue   red

7

8   7

bend it to the back (refer to page 27A)

mark and bend it to the back (refer to page 27A)

green

wire ②90cm

10

tadpole

small round beads

12

8

9

curved beads (curved beads used only for tadpole with legs)

large round   spangle

8

bend it to the back (refer to page 27A)

Animals in flocks

terrier✳ostrich✳pig✳cat D

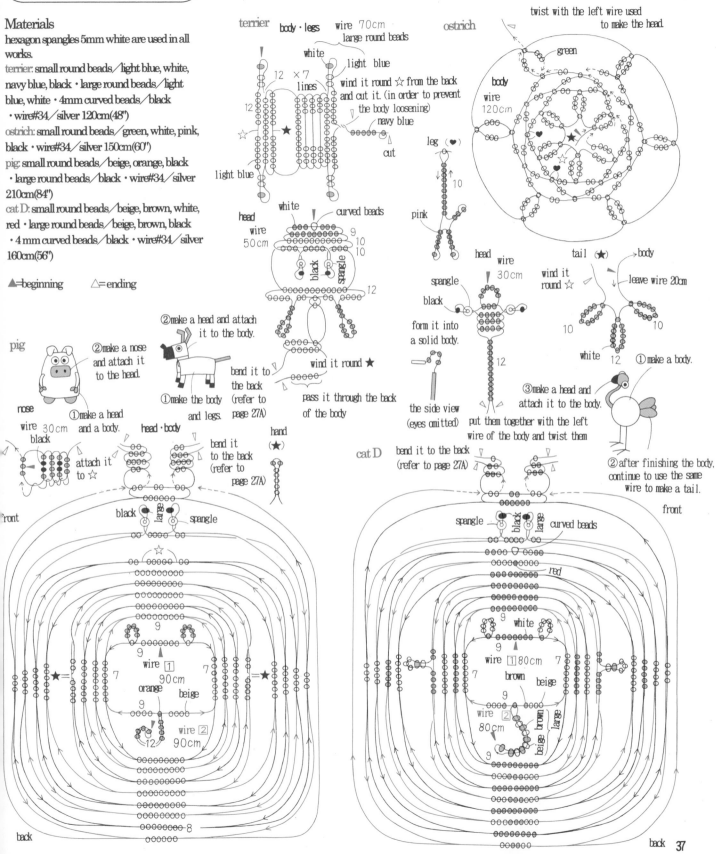

Materials

hexagon spangles 5mm white are used in all works.

terrier: small round beads／light blue, white, navy blue, black・large round beads／light blue, white・4mm curved beads／black ・wire#34／silver 120cm(48")

ostrich: small round beads／green, white, pink, black・wire#34／silver 150cm(60")

pig: small round beads／beige, orange, black ・large round beads／black・wire#34／silver 210cm(84")

cat D: small round beads／beige, brown, white, red・large round beads／beige, brown, black ・4mm curved beads／black・wire#34／silver 160cm(56")

▲=beginning   △=ending

terrier

body・legs   wire 70cm   large round beads

white
light blue

12 × 7 lines

12

☆

light blue

wind it round ☆ from the back and cut it. (in order to prevent the body loosening)

navy blue

cut

white   curved beads

head
wire 50cm

9
10
10

black   spangle

12

②make a head and attach it to the body.

bend it to the back (refer to page 27A)

①make the body and legs.

wind it round ★

pass it through the back of the body

pig

②make a nose and attach it to the head.

nose

①make a head and a body.

wire 30cm
black

head・body

attach it to ☆

bend it to the back (refer to page 27A)

hand (★)

ostrich

twist with the left wire used to make the head

green

body
wire 120cm

leg (♥)

10

pink

head   wire 30cm

spangle

black

form it into a solid body.

the side view (eyes omitted)

put them together with the left wire of the body and twist them

tail (★)   body

wind it round ☆

leave wire 20cm

10   10

white   12

①make a body.

③make a head and attach it to the body.

②after finishing the body, continue to use the same wire to make a tail.

cat D

bend it to the back (refer to page 27A)

spangle   black   large   curved beads

red

9   white

wire ①80cm   7

brown   beige

9

wire ②
80cm

beige brown   large

9

front

front

black   large   spangle

9

wire ①
90cm   7

orange   beige

9

wire ②
90cm

12

back   8

back   37

dachshund

Materials

dachshund: small round beads／beige, mixed color, black・large round beads／beige・4mm curved beads／black・5mm hexagon spangles／white・wire#34／silver 130cm(52")

▲=beginning   △=ending

②make a head and attach it
to the body.

①make a body and legs.

dachshund

large round beads beige

body・legs

12 ×11 lines

12

☆   ★

beige

mixed color

wire 80cm

wind it round ☆ from the back
and cut it. (in order to prevent
the body loosening)

cut here

head wire 50cm   curved bean

spangle
12   black

20   20

bend them to the back
(refer to page 27A)

wind it round

pass it through the back of the body.

house with red roof＊house with orange roof＊tree

Materials

house with red roof: small round beads／yellow green, red, white・wire#31／silver 400cm(160"), wire#34／silver 40cm(16")

house with orange roof: small round beads／orange, white, gray, dark brown・wire#31／silver 415cm(166")

tree(for one piece.< >different color. use same color of beads unless otherwise indicated) :small round beads／green<yellow green>, brown・wire#31／silver 70cm(28"), wire#34／silver 80cm(32")

▲=beginning   △=ending

②make the front of the roof with the wire 1.

①make the front, the back, 2 pieces of
the side of the house.

④make the back of the roof
with the wire 2.

③make a small part
of the roof and
attach it
to the roof.

⑤pass the wire through
the bottom line to
strengthen it.

house with red roof

back   wire #31
60cm   leave wire 3cm

small part of the roof
wire #34   attach to
40cm   the roof ★

attach to the roof ★

center
front

17 ×7 lines   put it together
with the beginning.
twist and bend
them to
the back.

side
wire #31
50cm

11 ×7
lines

roof

attach it to ♥

21 ×5 lines

attach it
to ♥

♥

wire ② #31 80cm

attach it
to ♡

21 ×6
lines

pass one end through
the front line,
twist and
cut it.

11 ×7 lines

attach it
to ♡

side
wire
#31
50cm

make 3 pieces
of the side

attach it
to ◇

red   attach
★ the small part
of the roof

attach it
to ◇

9

wire ① #31 80cm

17
×
7 lines

strengthening wire
(#31 20cm)

house with orange roof

front

pass it through ☆ of the side to attach them.
twist and bend them
to the back. (refer
to page 27A)

side
wire ① ②

put it together
with the end of
the front roof, twist
and bend them
to the back.

☆   wind back
around
to end

9
11
13
15

wire ② 40cm

orange

wire ② 40cm

15
×
9 lines

dark brown

white

gray

wire ①
60cm

①make the front
and 3 pieces
of the side.

15
×
9 lines

wire ① 60cm

②attach the top
of the roof.

③attach to
the next face.

leave wire 3cm

④pass the wire
through the bottom line.

put it together with
the beginning, twist
and bend them

tree

flower pot

wire #31

yellow
green

front   wire #31 60cm

white

10
×
13 lines

brown

green
<yellow green>

pass one end through
the front line, twist and cut it.
(refer to page 27B)

tree   31

wire #34

7

leave wire 5cm

twist

②make a tree
and put it
into the pot.

wind the beginni
round the left w
and form it.

①make a pot.

wind them together
and form them

Home and garden

house with yellow roof＊flower cart＊arch

Materials
house with yellow roof: small round beads／brown, yellow, navy blue・wire#31／silver 480cm(172"), wire#34／silver 50cm(20")

flower cart: small round beads／white, green, pink, orange・wire#31／silver 200cm(80"), wire#34／silver 50cm(20')

arch : small round beads／white, green, pink・wire#31／silver 640cm(134")

▲=beginning　△= ending

house with yellow roof

back　wire #31 110cm

strengthening wire (#31,20cm)
put it together with the beginning. twist and bend them to the back.
leave wire 3 cm

18 × 6 line

twist and bend them to the back.

side
wire #31,50cm
9 × 6 line

roof
wind back around to end

10 × 16 line

wire #31 70cm

attach it to ◇ of the roof.

yellow

attach it to ◇ of the roof.

sew 2 pieces of the roof together.

side
wire #31 50cm

sew 2 pieces of the roof together.

wire #31 70cm

9 × 6 line

wind back around to end.

10 × 16 line

front

18 × 6 line

twist and bend them to the back.
(refer to page 27A)　brown

navy blue
wire #31,110cm

arch

chimney
wire #34, 50cm

③ make 2 pieces of the roof and sew 2 pieces together.

④ attach the roof to the side.

⑥ make the chimney and attach it to the roof.

attach it to the roof

② make 2 pieces of the side and attach them to the front and the back.

① make the front and the back.

⑤ pass the strengthening wire through the bottom line.

flower
wire # 34

flower cart

② make the side and use the same wire to make the handle.

③ attach the side to the bottom

① make the bottom

④ make wheels and attach them at the boundary between the side and the bottom.

14　14　12　14　14　pink

green

8

twist and bend them to the back. (refer to page 27A)

side
wire # 31　handle　white
70cm　30
orange
5 × 30 line
△ attach it to the bottom.

arch　3 × 64 line

leaves　flower　pink
green

repeat the same as ☆ 15 times.

repeat the same as ★ 15 times.

wind leaves and flowers round the arch, twist and bend them to the back. (refer to page 27A)

leaves, flower wire 100cm pass one end through the front line, twist and cut it. (refer to page 27B)

attach it to the bottom.

white
wire 100cm
arch

wheel　wire #31, 30cm ×2
make 2 pieces.

bottom　wire #31
70cm

attach them to the bottom.

③ make fences and attach them to the arch.

② make leaves and flowers wind them round the arch

① make a arch.

wire ② 20cm ×2

fence
make 2 set

wire ① 40cm ×10　make 10 pieces

pass it through ◆ and attach it.

attach it at the boundary between the side and the bottom.

10 × 10 line

pass one end through the front line, twist and cut it.

pass it through ◇ and attach it.

39

Home and garden   shop✳church✳chair✳table

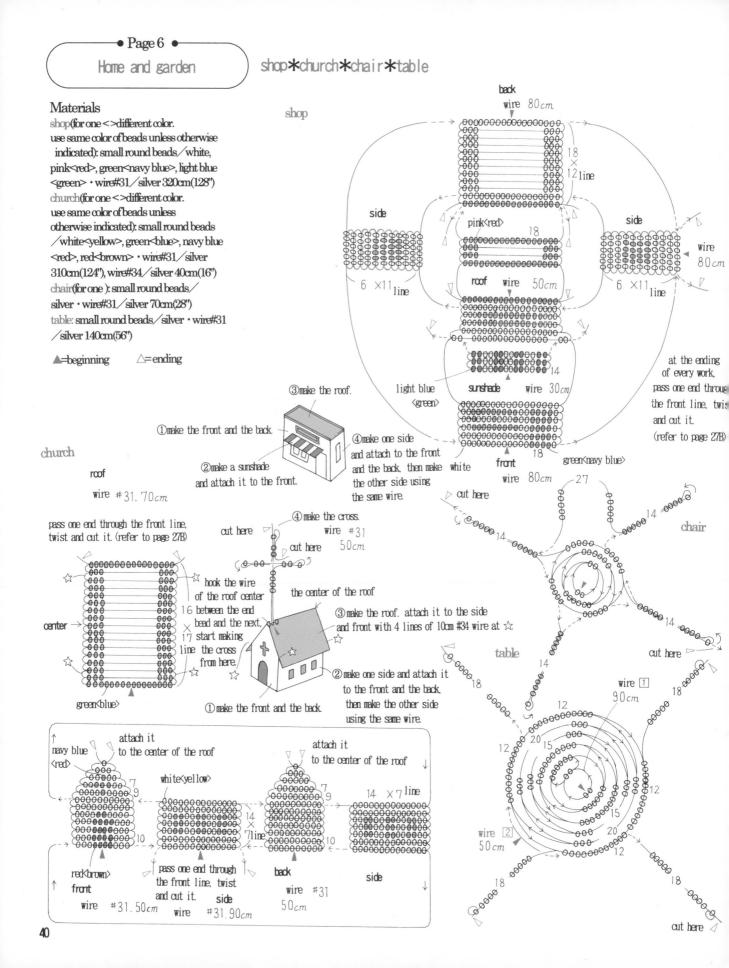

Materials

shop(for one <>different color.
use same color of beads unless otherwise
indicated): small round beads／white,
pink<red>, green<navy blue>, light blue
<green>・wire#31／silver 320cm(128")
church(for one <>different color.
use same color of beads unless
otherwise indicated): small round beads
／white<yellow>, green<blue>, navy blue
<red>, red<brown>・wire#31／silver
310cm(124"), wire#34／silver 40cm(16")
chair(for one): small round beads／
silver・wire#31／silver 70cm(28")
table: small round beads／silver・wire#31
／silver 140cm(56")

▲=beginning   △= ending

shop

back
wire 80cm

18
×
12 line

side   pink<red>   side
6 ×11 line   18   6 ×11 line
wire 80cm

roof   wire 50cm

light blue <green>

sunshade   wire 30cm   14

front   wire 80cm

green<navy blue>

at the ending
of every work,
pass one end through
the front line, twist
and cut it.
(refer to page 27B)

③make the roof.

①make the front and the back.
②make a sunshade and attach it to the front.
④make one side and attach to the front and the back, then make the other side using the same wire.

white

church

roof
wire #31. 70cm

pass one end through the front line,
twist and cut it. (refer to page 27B)

center

green<blue>

④make the cross.
wire #31 50cm

cut here   cut here

hook the wire
of the roof center
between the end
bead and the next,
start making
the cross
from here.

16
×
17 line

the center of the roof

③make the roof. attach it to the side
and front with 4 lines of 10cm #34 wire at ☆
②make one side and attach it
to the front and the back,
then make the other side
using the same wire.
①make the front and the back.

chair

cut here

27   14

14   14

table

cut here

18

wire ①
90cm

18

12

12
20
15

12

15

wire ②
50cm

20

12

18   18

cut here

navy blue <red>
attach it
to the center of the roof

white<yellow>

attach it
to the center of the roof

14 ×7 line

7
9

7
9

14
×
7 line

10   10

red<brown>
front
wire #31.50cm

pass one end through
the front line, twist
and cut it.   side
wire #31.90cm

back
wire #31
50cm

side

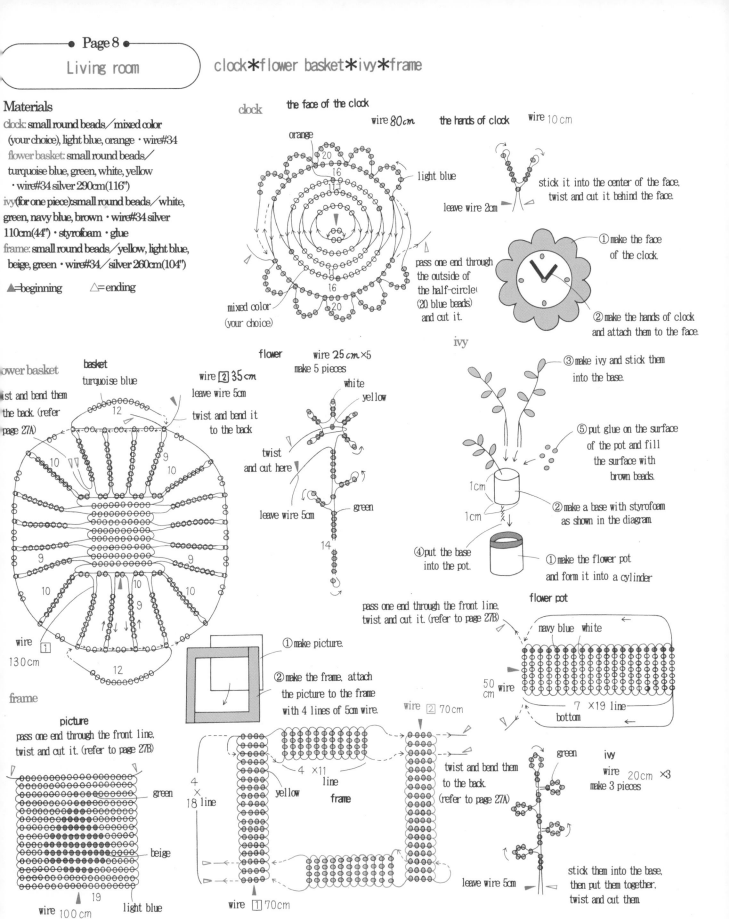

Materials

clock: small round beads／mixed color (your choice), light blue, orange ・wire#34
flower basket: small round beads／turquoise blue, green, white, yellow ・wire#34 silver 290cm(116")
ivy(for one piece):small round beads／white, green, navy blue, brown ・wire#34 silver 110cm(44") ・styrofoam ・glue
frame: small round beads／yellow, light blue, beige, green ・wire#34／silver 260cm(104")

▲=beginning △=ending

clock the face of the clock
wire 80cm the hands of clock wire 10cm
orange
light blue
stick it into the center of the face, twist and cut it behind the face.
leave wire 2cm
pass one end through the outside of the half-circle (20 blue beads) and cut it.
mixed color (your choice)

① make the face of the clock.
② make the hands of clock and attach them to the face.
③ make ivy and stick them into the base.
⑤ put glue on the surface of the pot and fill the surface with brown beads.
② make a base with styrofoam as shown in the diagram.
④ put the base into the pot.
① make the flower pot and form it into a cylinder

flower basket
basket turquoise blue
twist and bend them the back. (refer page 27A)
wire ② 35cm leave wire 5cm twist and bend it to the back
flower wire 25cm×5 make 5 pieces
white yellow
twist and cut here
leave wire 5cm
green
leave wire 5cm
wire ① 130cm

flower pot
pass one end through the front line, twist and cut it. (refer to page 27B)
navy blue white
50cm wire
7 ×19 line
bottom

frame
picture
pass one end through the front line, twist and cut it. (refer to page 27B)
green beige light blue
wire 100cm 19

① make picture.
② make the frame, attach the picture to the frame with 4 lines of 5cm wire.
4 ×11 line yellow
wire ② 70cm
twist and bend them to the back. (refer to page 27A)
frame
4 ×18 line
wire ① 70cm

ivy green
wire 20cm ×3 make 3 pieces
stick them into the base, then put them together, twist and cut them.
leave wire 5cm

cupboard ✳teddy bear✳cushion✳palm tree

Materials

cupboard : small round beads／blue, yellow
・wire#34／silver 480cm(192")

teddy bear(for one <>different color.
use same color of beads unless otherwise
indicated): small round beads／dark brown
<brown>, beige・large round beads／black
・wire#31／silver 60cm(24")

cushion(for one <>different color.
use same color of beads unless otherwise
indicated): small round beads／pink<light
blue>, light blue<pink>・wire#34／silver
50cm(20")

palm tree: small round beads／green, orange,
yellow・large round beads／dark brown
・wire#34／silver 410cm(164")・styrofoam
・glue

▲=beginning   △=ending

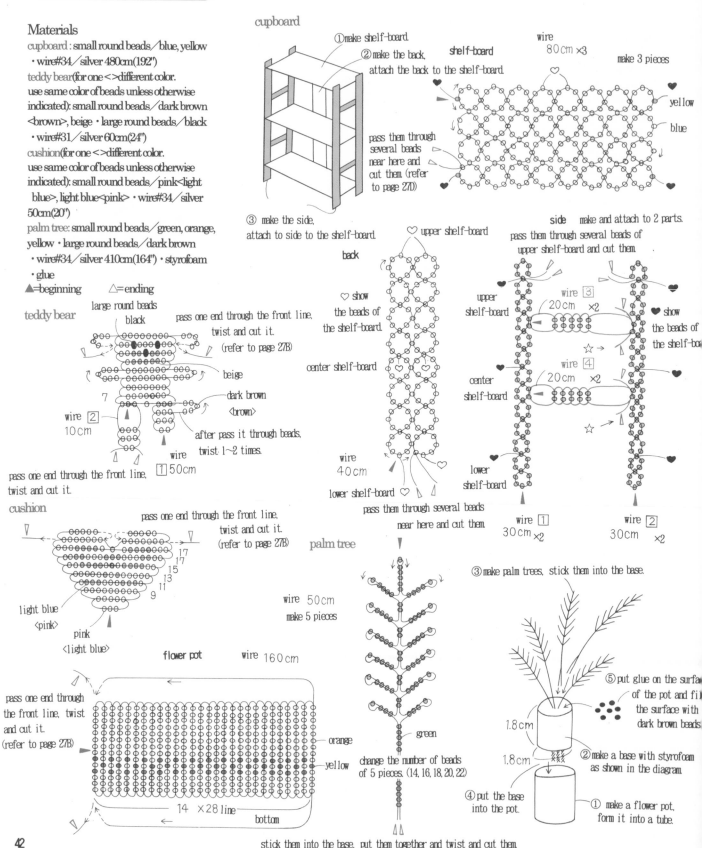

cupboard

① make shelf-board.

② make the back,
attach the back to the shelf-board.

pass them through
several beads
near here and
cut them (refer
to page 27D)

③ make the side,
attach to side to the shelf-board.

shelf-board

wire
80cm ×3

make 3 pieces

yellow

blue

teddy bear

large round beads
black

pass one end through the front line,
twist and cut it.
(refer to page 27B)

beige

dark brown
<brown>

wire ② 10cm

after pass it through beads,
twist 1~2 times.

7

wire ① 50cm

pass one end through the front line,
twist and cut it.

cushion

pass one end through the front line,
twist and cut it.
(refer to page 27B)

17
17
15
13
11
9

light blue
<pink>

pink
<light blue>

flower pot   wire 160cm

pass one end through
the front line, twist
and cut it.
(refer to page 27B)

orange

yellow

14 ×28 line

bottom

♡ upper shelf-board

back

♡ show
the beads of
the shelf-board.

center shelf-board

wire
40cm

lower shelf-board ♡

pass them through several beads
near here and cut them

palm tree

side   make and attach to 2 parts.

pass them through several beads of
upper shelf-board and cut them

upper
shelf-board

wire ③
20cm ×2

☆ →

wire ④
20cm ×2

center
shelf-board

☆ →

lower
shelf-board

wire ①
30cm ×2

show
the beads of
the shelf-board

wire ②
30cm ×2

wire 50cm
make 5 pieces

green

change the number of beads
of 5 pieces. (14, 16, 18, 20, 22)

stick them into the base, put them together and twist and cut them

③ make palm trees, stick them into the base.

⑤ put glue on the surface
of the pot and fill
the surface with
dark brown beads

1.8cm

② make a base with styrofoam
as shown in the diagram.

1.8cm

④ put the base
into the pot.

① make a flower pot,
form it into a tube.

table✳desk light✳sofa

Materials

table: small round beads／pink, yellow・wire #34／silver 150cm(60″)・instant glue

desk light: small round beads／yellow green, yellow, pink・wire#34／silver 100cm(40″)

sofa: small round beads／red・wire#31／silver 300cm(120″)

▲=beginning   △=ending

table

tabletop

pass one end through the front line, twist and cut it. (refer to page 27B)

① make a tabletop.

7
9
23
24
23
21
19
17
14
10

yellow
pink

wire 100cm

legs

wire 50cm

② make legs and attach them to the tabletop.
pass them through ♡ and cut them.

leave wire 5cm

18   18

12   12

18

desk light

lampshade
wire 60cm

pink
yellow green

s it through ♡ and cut

7
7
★
leave the wire 5cm
♡
7
♡

pass it through ♥ and cut it when finished.

base
wire 40cm

pass them through the center of the lampshade and cut.

★   ☆

① make a lampshade.

② make a base and attach it to the lampshade.

yellow

sofa

side

wire ②40cm
left   leave wire 5cm

wire ①
170cm

twist and bend them to the back.
(refer to page 27A)

① make the side.

make a seat picking up beads of the side.

back
10

10   10

10   10

10

○ show the beads you pick up to attach the seat to the side.

pass it through ♡ and cut it.

right

♡   ♡

seat
wire 90cm

twist and bend them to the back.

Afternoon on the street girl A · B ✽ boy ✽ flower cart

Materials

girl B: small round beads／white, dark brown, navy blue · large round beads／white · 3mm curved beads／navy blue, yellow · 5mm pearl beads／white · wire#34／bronze 80cm(32″)

girl A: small round beads／white, dark brown, pink · large round beads／white, orange · 3mm curved beads／orange, clear · 5mm pearl beads／white · wire#34／bronze 80cm (32″)

boy: small round beads／white, dark brown, light blue, green · large round beads／green, white · 3mm curved beads／green, blue · 5mm pearl beads／white · wire#31／bronze 60cm(24″)

flower cart: small round beads／white, red, dark brown, green, pink, beige, yellow · large round beads／white · 3mm pearl beads／gold · wire#31／bronze 570cm(228″)

▲=beginning   △=ending

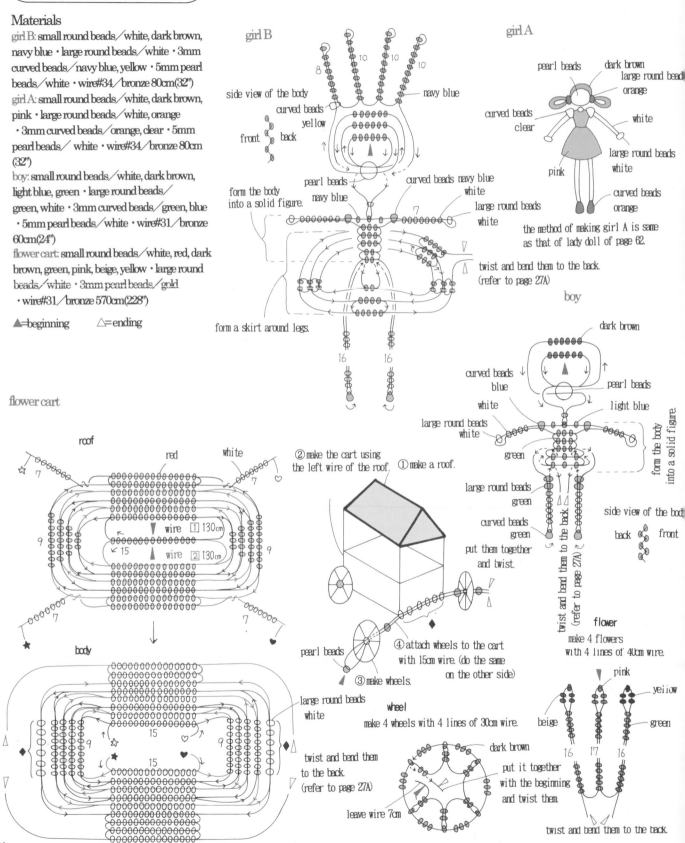

girl B

8 10 10 10

side view of the body

curved beads

yellow

front back

navy blue

form the body into a solid figure.

pearl beads

navy blue

curved beads navy blue

white

large round beads

white

7

form a skirt around legs.

16 16

girl A

pearl beads dark brown

large round beads

orange

curved beads

clear

white

large round beads

white

pink

curved beads

orange

the method of making girl A is same as that of lady doll of page 62.

twist and bend them to the back. (refer to page 27A)

boy

dark brown

curved beads

blue

white

large round beads

white

green

large round beads

green

curved beads

green

pearl beads

light blue

form the body into a solid figure.

side view of the body

back front

twist and bend them to the back. (refer to page 27A)

twist and bend them to the back.

flower

make 4 flowers with 4 lines of 40cm wire.

pink

yellow

beige

green

16 17 16

flower cart

roof

☆ 7

red

white

7 ♡

wire ① 130cm

← 15

wire ② 130cm

9

9

7

7

★

♥

② make the cart using the left wire of the roof.

① make a roof.

put them together and twist.

④ attach wheels to the cart with 15cm wire. (do the same on the other side)

pearl beads

③ make wheels.

large round beads white

wheel

make 4 wheels with 4 lines of 30cm wire.

twist and bend them to the back. (refer to page 27A)

dark brown

put it together with the beginning and twist them

leave wire 7cm

body

large round beads white

△ ◆ ☆

9

15

♡ 9

◆ △

15

♥

△ △

44

Afternoon on the street

street lamp✱tree✱table✱chair flower

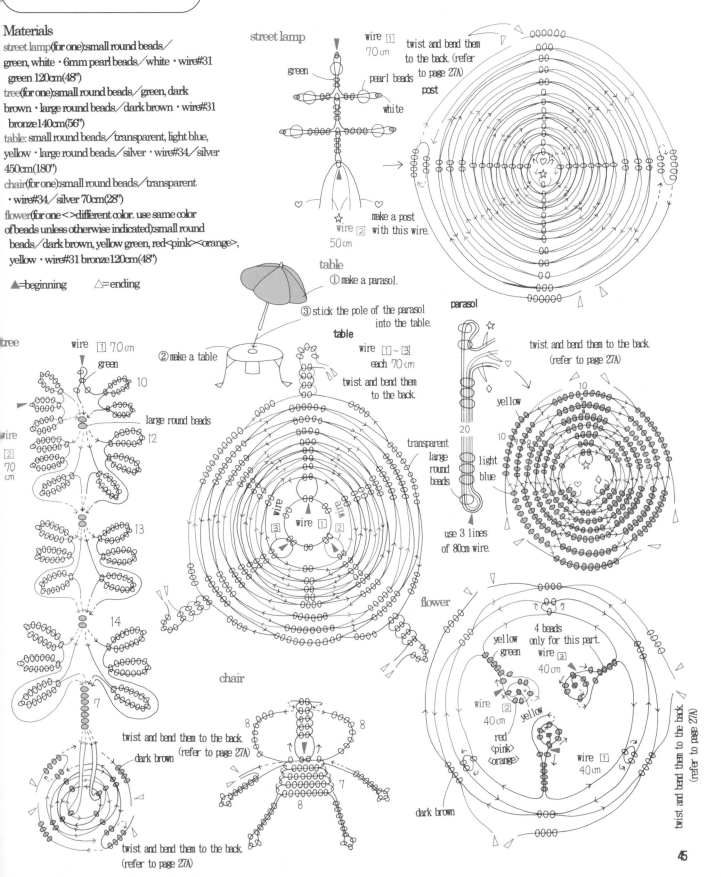

Materials

street lamp(for one):small round beads/
green, white・6mm pearl beads/white・wire#31
green 120cm(48")
tree(for one):small round beads/green, dark
brown・large round beads/dark brown・wire#31
bronze140cm(56")
table: small round beads/transparent, light blue,
yellow・large round beads/silver・wire#34/silver
450cm(180")
chair(for one):small round beads/transparent
・wire#34/silver 70cm(28")
flower(for one <>different color. use same color
of beads unless otherwise indicated):small round
beads/dark brown, yellow green, red<pink><orange>,
yellow・wire#31 bronze120cm(48")

▲=beginning △=ending

street lamp

green
pearl beads
white
☆ wire ② 50cm
wire ① 70cm
twist and bend them to the back. (refer to page 27A)
post
make a post with this wire.

table
① make a parasol.
② make a table
③ stick the pole of the parasol into the table.

parasol
☆
twist and bend them to the back. (refer to page 27A)
yellow
light blue
transparent large round beads
20 10 10
use 3 lines of 80cm wire.

table
wire ①~③ each 70cm
twist and bend them to the back.
wire ②
arm
wire ①
③ wire
large round beads

tree
wire ① 70cm
green
10
12
large round beads
wire ② 70cm
13
14
7
twist and bend them to the back. (refer to page 27A)
dark brown
twist and bend them to the back. (refer to page 27A)

chair
8 8
8
7
8

flower
yellow green
4 beads only for this part.
wire ③ 40cm
wire ② 40cm
yellow
red <pink> <orange>
wire ① 40cm
dark brown
twist and bend them to the back. (refer to page 27A)

45

Afternoon on the street   fountain✱bicycle✱traffic sign A・B✱traffic lights

Materials

fountain: small round beads／clear, blue, white・4mm curved beads／clear・wire#34／silver 270cm(108")

bicycle: small round beads／orange, silver, black・large round beads／orange, white・3mm pearl beads／silver・wire#31／silver・100cm(40"), wire#34／silver 60cm(24")

traffic sign A: small round beads／white, navy blue・wire#34／silver 60cm(24")

traffic sign B: small round beads／white, red, light blue・wire#31／bronze 60cm(24")

traffic lights: small round beads／gray, black, red, green・wire#34／silver 60cm(24")

▲=beginning   △=ending

fountain

center part

wire ① 90cm

wire ②③

make in the same way with wire 2,3. (90cm each)

curved beads

clear

15 20 15

bend them outside.

①make the center part

white

blue

②make the rest with the wire of the center part.

twist and bend them to the back. (refer to page 27A)

bicycle

wheel

make 2 wheels with 2 lines of 30cm wire.

black

silver

leave wire 7cm

put it together with the beginning and twist them

Body

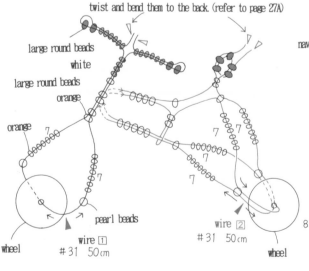

twist and bend them to the back. (refer to page 27A)

large round beads

white

large round beads

orange

orange

7

pearl beads

wheel

wire ①
#31 50cm

7 7

7

7

wire ②
#31 50cm

wheel

traffic sign A

navy blue

8
10
12
10
8

white   lines

2

×
12

8

twist and bend them to the back. (refer to page 27A)

traffic sign B

light blue

8
10
12

red

2

×
12

white   lines

8

twist and bend them to the back.

Traffic lights

8

black

red

green

2

×
12

gray   lines

8

twist and bend them to the back.

strawberry✳mushroom✳cherry✳pineapple✳watermelon✳sweet pepper

Materials

strawberry: small round beads／red, black, green・wire#34／silver 120cm(48")

mushroom(for one <>different color. use same color of beads unless otherwise indicated):small round beads／white<beige>, brown・wire#31／silver 50cm(20")

cherry(for one <>different color. use same color of beads unless otherwise indicated) small round beads／pink<red>,yellow green ・wire#31／silver 120cm(48")

pineapple: small round beads／orange, green, brown・wire#31／silver 120cm(48")

watermelon: small round beads／red, green, white, black・wire#31／silver 100cm(40")

sweet pepper(for one <>different color. use same color of beads unless otherwise indicated):small round beads／red <yellow><green>, green・wire#31／silver 70cm(28")

▲=beginning   △=ending

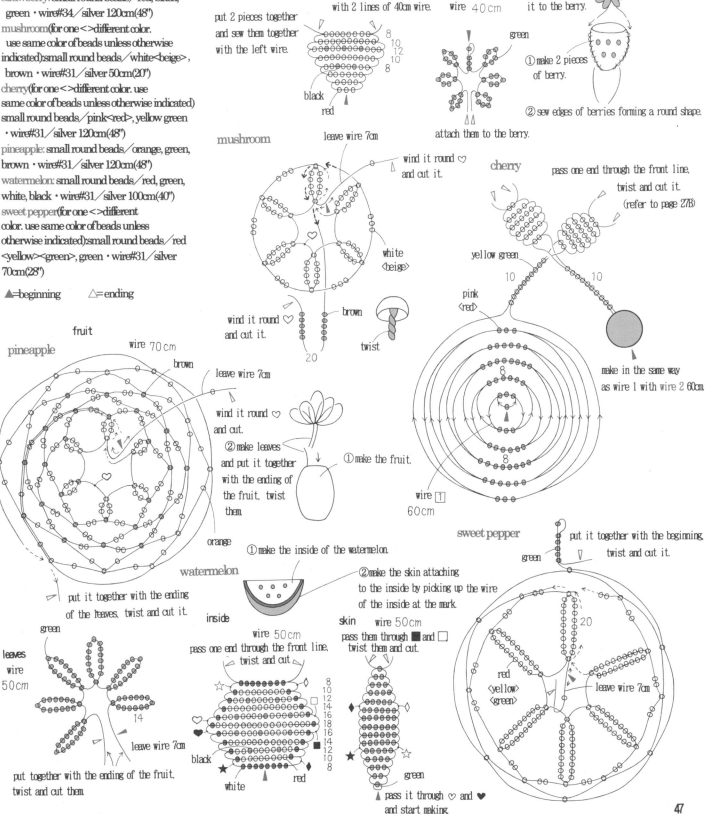

strawberry

berry   make 2 pieces with 2 lines of 40cm wire.

put 2 pieces together and sew them together with the left wire.

8
10
12
10
8

black
red

leave wire 7cm

calyx
wire 40cm

green

③make calyx and attach it to the berry.

①make 2 pieces of berry.

②sew edges of berries forming a round shape.

attach them to the berry.

mushroom

wind it round ♡ and cut it.

white <beige>

wind it round ♡ and cut it.

brown

20

twist

cherry

pass one end through the front line, twist and cut it. (refer to page 27B)

yellow green
10   10

pink <red>

8

8

wire ① 60cm

make in the same way as wire 1 with wire 2 60cm

pineapple

fruit   wire 70cm

brown

leave wire 7cm

wind it round ♡ and cut.

②make leaves and put it together with the ending of the fruit, twist them

①make the fruit.

orange

put it together with the ending of the leaves, twist and cut it.

leaves
wire 50cm

green

14

leave wire 7cm

put together with the ending of the fruit, twist and cut them

watermelon

①make the inside of the watermelon.

②make the skin attaching to the inside by picking up the wire of the inside at the mark.

inside   wire 50cm
pass one end through the front line, twist and cut

☆
◇
8
10
12
14
16
18
16
14
12
10
8

♡

□

black

■

★

white   red

skin   wire 50cm
pass them through ■ and □ twist them and cut.

◆
◇
◆
8
10
12
14
14
12
10
8

★

green

◇

▲ pass it through ♡ and ♥ and start making

sweet pepper

green

put it together with the beginning, twist and cut it.

20

red <yellow> <green>

leave wire 7cm

47

Vegetables and fruits

carrot✳corn✳spinach✳grapes

Materials

carrot: small round beads／orange, green
 ・wire#31／silver 140cm(56")
corn: small round beads／beige, green, white
 ・wire#31／silver 135cm(54")
spinach(for one):small round beads／
green, red ・wire#31／silver 70cm(28")
grapes(for one bunch.<>different color. use
same color of beads unless otherwise indicated)
:small round beads／green ・large round beads
／navy blue<violet> ・wire#31／silver 70cm(28")

▲=beginning   △= ending

carrot

root make 2 pieces
with 2 lines of 50cm wire.
leave the wire a little
to sew 2 pieces together.

8

10
8

orange

leaves   wire 40cm

green

14

leave wire 5cm

attach it to the root.

③make leaves and attach them to the root.

①make 2 pieces
of root

②sew edges
of 2 roots together.
and cut it.
(refer to page 27B)

grapes

green   pass one end through
the front line, twis

8

large round beads
navy blue
<violet>

twist them to form
into the shape
of grapes.

wire 70cm

corn

corn   wire 70cm

beige

leave wire 5cm
after making the corn.
wind it round ♡
and cut.

19
(★)
white
pass through
1～3 among
19 beads.

wind it round ♥
and cut it.

9
green

leaves   wire 60cm

7 ×5 line

attach them to the corn.

attach them
to the corn with 5cm wire.

②make leaves and attach them to it.

①make the corn.

attach them to it with the ending of leaves.

spinach

25

25

25

25

25

green

red

twist and cut them

twist them

Bread and sweets

croissant✳twist bread

Materials

croissant(for one):small round beads／
beige, brown ・wire#34／gold 70cm(28")
twist bread: small round beads／beige
 ・wire#34／gold 50cm(20")
▲=beginning   △= ending

croissant

pass them through ☆ and cut. (refer to page 27D)

brown

8
9
10
11
12
14
16
18

beige

roll up from the beginning.
pass the ending through ☆
and cut it.

twist bread

after putting 3 lines of beads together and twist,
form them into a twist bread and cut the ending.

○○○○○25 ○○○25 ○○○○○
○○○○○25 ○○○25 ○○○○○
○○○○○25 ○○○25 ○○○○○

center

①pass beads through the wire
and put 3 lines together
and twist them

②fold it at the center
and twist them to form it into the twist bread.

48

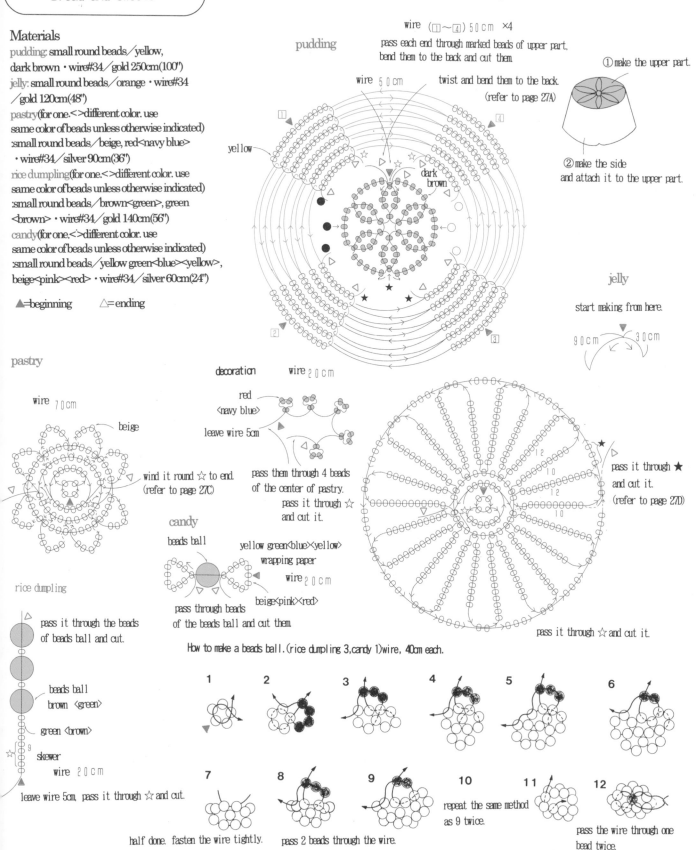

Page 14

Bread and sweets

pudding✳jelly✳pastry✳rice dumpling✳candy

Materials

pudding: small round beads／yellow, dark brown・wire#34／gold 250cm(100")

jelly: small round beads／orange・wire#34／gold 120cm(48")

pastry(for one.<>different color. use same color of beads unless otherwise indicated) :small round beads／beige, red<navy blue>・wire#34／silver 90cm(36")

rice dumpling(for one.<>different color. use same color of beads unless otherwise indicated) :small round beads／brown<green>, green<brown>・wire#34／gold 140cm(56")

candy(for one.<>different color. use same color of beads unless otherwise indicated) :small round beads／yellow green<blue><yellow>, beige<pink><red>・wire#34／silver 60cm(24")

▲=beginning   △= ending

pudding

wire (①～④)50cm ×4

pass each end through marked beads of upper part. bend them to the back and cut them.

wire 50cm

twist and bend them to the back. (refer to page 27A)

yellow

dark brown

①make the upper part.

②make the side and attach it to the upper part.

jelly

start making from here.

90cm   30cm

pastry

wire 70cm

beige

wind it round ☆ to end. (refer to page 27C)

decoration

wire 20cm

red <navy blue>

leave wire 5cm

pass them through 4 beads of the center of pastry. pass it through ☆ and cut it.

pass it through ★ and cut it. (refer to page 27D)

pass it through ☆ and cut it.

candy

beads ball

yellow green<blue><yellow> wrapping paper

wire 20cm

beige<pink><red>

pass through beads of the beads ball and cut them.

rice dumpling

pass it through the beads of beads ball and cut.

beads ball brown <green>

green <brown>

skewer wire 20cm

leave wire 5cm, pass it through ☆ and cut.

How to make a beads ball.(rice dumpling 3, candy 1)wire, 40cm each.

1
2
3
4
5
6

7   half done. fasten the wire tightly.

8   pass 2 beads through the wire.

9

10   repeat the same method as 9 twice.

11

12   pass the wire through one bead twice.

49

Bread and sweets

French bread✱doughnut✱chocolate cake✱Swiss roll✱fish-shape cake
(taiyaki)

Materials

French bread: small round beads／
orange, brown・wire#34／gold
50cm(20″)

doughnut: small round beads／brown
・wire#34／silver 100cm(40″)

chocolate cake: small round beads／
dark brown, brown, cream・wire#34
／gold 150cm(60″)

Swiss roll: small round beads／beige,
cream, orange・wire#34／gold 210cm(84″)

fish-shape cake: small round beads／
beige, brown・wire#34／gold 100cm(40″)

▲=beginning   △=ending

French bread

pass one end through the front line,
twist and cut it. (refer to page 27B)

brown

orange ▲

doughnut

pass one end through the front line,
twist and cut it. (refer to page 27B)

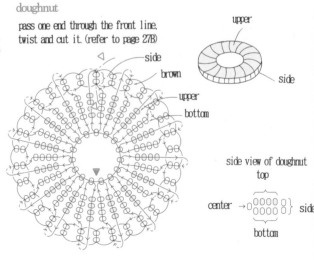

upper

side

brown

upper

bottom

side

side view of doughnut
top

center →o 0000 } side

bottom

chocolate cake

upper part, back
wire 70cm

8 ×

11 line

8 ×

11 line

pass it through
the back to end.

brown

wire 70cm

side
12 ×6 line

dark brown

pass it through the side to end.
(refer to page 27D)

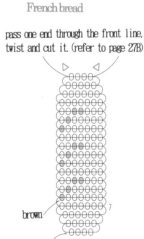

decoration   wire 10cm

cream

stick it into the upper part,
twist in the back.

③make the decoration
and attach it to the top.

①make the upper part
and the back

②make the side picking up
the wire of the upper part.

Swiss roll

back

wire 60cm

cream

orange

side
wire 90cm

wind it up to end.

beige

front
wire 60cm

☆ pass one end through
the front line, twist
and cut it.
(refer to page 27B)

① make the front and the back

② make the side picking up
the wire of the front
and the back.

fish-shape cake(taiyaki)

head

brown   beige

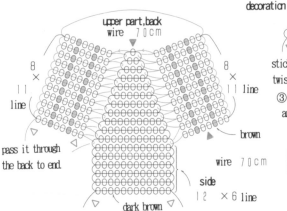

center

wind it up to end.

head

center

Restaurant — hamburg steak✱egg sunny-side up✱deep-fried shrimp✱omelet

Materials

hamburg steak [plate(small size)]:small round beads／white・wire#34／silver 210cm(84″) [hamburg steak]:small round beads／dark brown・wire#31／bronze 50cm(20″) [French fries]:small round beads／beige・wire#31／bronze 45cm(18″) [parsley]:small round beads／green・wire#31／green 40cm(16″)

egg sunny-side up [plate(small size)]:small round beads／navy blue・wire#34／silver 210cm(84″) [egg sunny-side up]:small round beads／white, yellow・wire#34／silver 120cm(48″) [sausage]:large round beads／orange・wire#31／bronze 10cm(4″) [parsley]:small round beads／green・wire#31／green 40cm(16″)

deep fried shrimp [plate(small size)]:small round beads／white・wire#34／silver 210cm(84″) [deep-fried shrimp]:small round beads／orange, red・wire#31／bronze 200cm(80″) [parsley]:small round beads／green・wire#31／green 40cm(16″)

omelet [plate(small size)]:small round beads／light blue・wire#34／silver 210cm(84″) [omelet]:small round beads／yellow・wire#31／bronze 80cm(32″) [ketchup]:small round beads／red・wire#31／bronze 20cm(8″) [parsley]:small round beads／green・wire#31／green 40cm(16″)

▲=beginning   △= ending

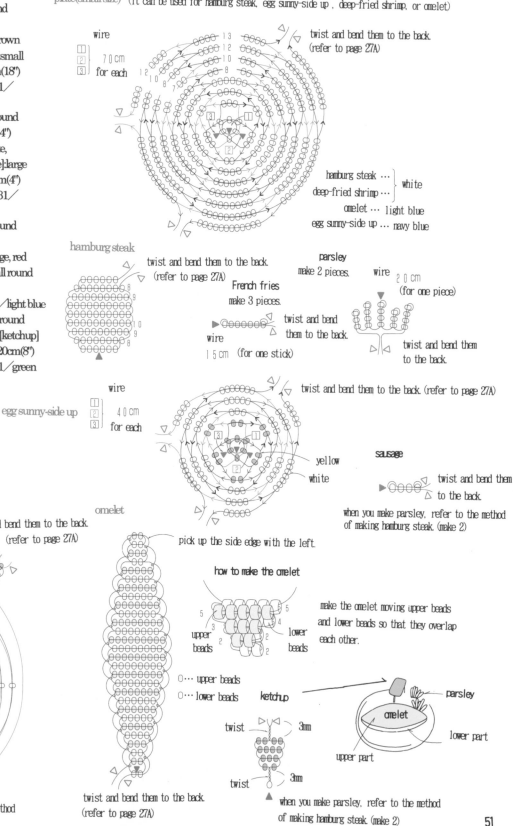

plate(small size) (it can be used for hamburg steak, egg sunny-side up, deep-fried shrimp, or omelet)

wire
① ② ③ 70cm for each

twist and bend them to the back. (refer to page 27A)

hamburg steak … / deep-fried shrimp … } white / omelet … light blue / egg sunny-side up … navy blue

hamburg steak

twist and bend them to the back. (refer to page 27A)

parsley make 2 pieces.

wire 20cm (for one piece)

French fries make 3 pieces.

twist and bend them to the back.

wire 15cm (for one stick)

twist and bend them to the back.

egg sunny-side up

wire ① ② ③ 40cm for each

twist and bend them to the back. (refer to page 27A)

yellow / white

sausage

twist and bend them to the back.

when you make parsley, refer to the method of making hamburg steak. (make 2)

omelet

pick up the side edge with the left.

how to make the omelet

upper beads / lower beads

make the omelet moving upper beads and lower beads so that they overlap each other.

○… upper beads
○… lower beads

ketchup

twist 3mm

twist 3mm

▲ when you make parsley, refer to the method of making hamburg steak. (make 2)

parsley / omelet / lower part / upper part

twist and bend them to the back. (refer to page 27A)

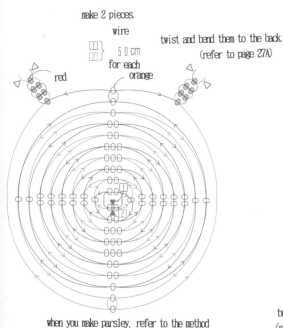

deep-fried shrimp

make 2 pieces.

wire ① ② 50cm for each

red / orange

twist and bend them to the back. (refer to page 27A)

when you make parsley, refer to the method of making hamburg steak. (make 2)

Restaurant

spaghetti✳lunch for children✳salad✳spoon✳fork✳knife

Materials

spaghetti [plate(large size)]:small round beads／white・wire#34／silver 300cm(120″) [spaghetti]:small round beads／orange・large round beads／green, orange, dark brown・wire#31／bronze 90cm (36″)

lunch for children [plate(large size)]:small round beads／white・wire#34／silver 300cm(120″) [chicken rice]:small round beads／orange, white, red, green・wire#31／bronze 100cm(40″) [cake]:small round beads／beige, pink, green・4mm curved beads／red・wire#31／bronze 90cm(36″) [hamburg steak]:small round beads／dark brown・wire#31／bronze 40cm(16″) [parsley]:small round beads／green・wire#31／green 40cm(16″) [sausage]:large round beads／orange・wire#31／bronze 10cm(4″)

salad [salad bowl]:small round beads／clear・wire#34／silver 140cm(56″) [lettuce]:small round beads／transparent, yellow green・wire#34／silver 150cm(60″) [asparagus]:small round beads／green・wire#31／green 40cm(16″) [mini-tomato]:small round beads／green, red・5.5mm special large／red・wire#31／bronze 60cm(24″)

spoon: small round beads／silver・wire#34／silver 40cm(16″)

fork: small round beads／silver・wire#34／silver 40cm(16″)

knife: small round beads／silver・wire#34／silver 40cm(16″)

▲=beginning　△= ending

plate(large size) (it can be used for spaghetti, lunch for children)

wire
1
2 } 100cm
3   for each

twist and bend them to the back. (refer to page 27A)

lunch for children

spaghetti
wind it up to form spaghetti so that it looks delicious on the plate.

small round bead orange

large round bead green

large round bead orange

large round bead dark brown

repeat the same method as ☆ 6 times.

twist and bend them to the back.

chicken rice

orange
white
red

wire
1
2 } 50cm
for each

green

cake　sponge cake
beige
pink

wire
1
2 } 40cm
for each

decoration

twist and bend them to the back.

wire 10cm
curved beads
green

wind round ▲ of sponge cake and cu

hamburg steak

twist and bend them to the back.

twist and bend them to the back. (refer to page 27A)

when you make parsley, refer to the method of making hamburg steak.
when you make sausage, refer to the method of making deep-fried shrimp.

salad　　salad bowl
twist and bend them to the back. (refer to page 27A)
wire
1
2 } 70cm

side

bottom

side

side

side

asparagus

13　15　13

twist and bend them to the back.

bottom

side

bend the edge a little bit.

lettuce
make 3 leaves.

yellow green
transparent

wire 50cm (for 1 leaf)

mini-tomato
make 2 pieces.

wire 30cm (for 1 piece)

green
special large red
red

twist and bend them to the back.

twist and bend them to the back.

spoon

7

twist and bend to the back. (refer to page

fork

twist and bend t to the back.

knife

twist and bend them to the back

52

Restaurant

sushi✳onigiri(rice ball)✳noodles✳chopsticks

Materials

sushi [wooden plate]:small round beads／beige
・wire#31／bronze 330cm(132″) [hosomaki]:small
round beads／black, white, dark brown, green,pink
・wire#31／bronze 70cm(28″) [futomaki]:small
round beads／black, white, dark brown, green,
pink・wire#31／bronze 90cm(36″) [Japanese omelet]
small round beads／yellow, black・wire#31／bronze
35cm(14″) [prawn]:small round beads／red, white,
beige, orange・wire#31／bronze 35cm(14″) [sushi
rice]:small round beads／white・wire#34／silver
40cm(48″)
onigiri(rice ball) [leaf]:small round beads／green
・wire#31／green 90cm(36″) [nori-onigiri]:small round
beads／white, black・wire#34／silver 100cm(40″)
ume-onigiri:small round beads／white, cream, red
・wire#34／silver 100cm(40″) [takuan(Japanese
pickled radish)]:small round beads／yellow・wire#31
／silver 40cm(16″)
noodles [bowl]:small round beads／light purple, gray
・wire#34／silver 270cm(108″) [noodle]:small round
beads／white・wire#31／bronze 90cm(36″) [food]:small
round beads／brown, pink, white, green・wire#31／
bronze 45cm(18″)
chopsticks: small round beads／red, pink・wire#31／
bronze 40cm(16″)
▲=beginning   △=ending

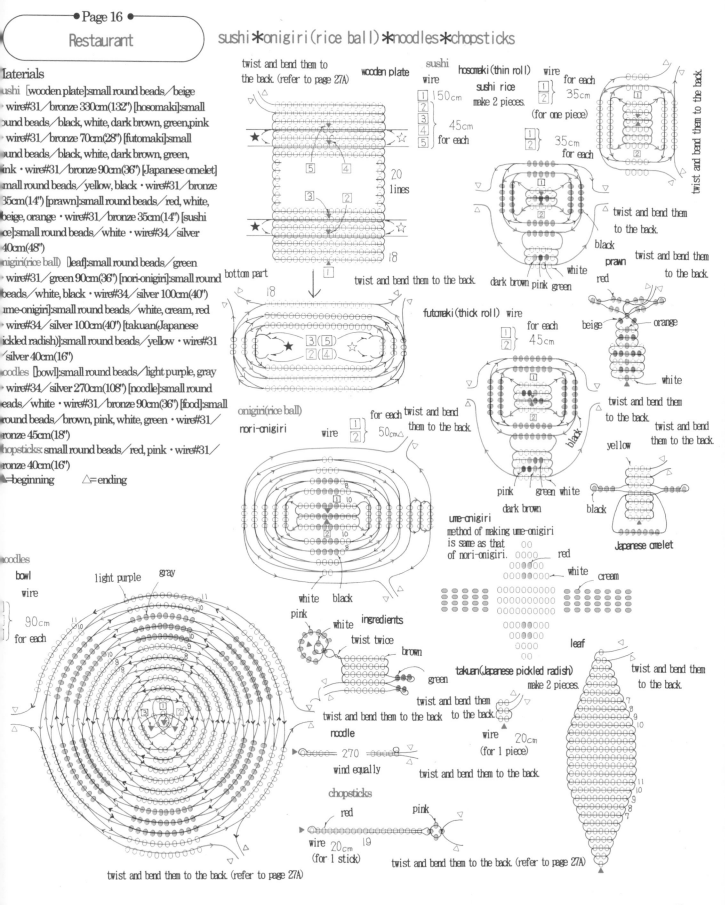

twist and bend them to
the back. (refer to page 27A)
wooden plate

sushi

hosomaki (thin roll) wire
sushi rice   ①②} for each 35cm
make 2 pieces.   (for one piece)
①② } 35cm for each

twist and bend them to the back.

wire ① 150cm ②③④⑤ 45cm for each

20 lines

18

bottom part

twist and bend them to the back.

twist and bend them
to the back.

black
white
dark brown pink green

prawn   twist and bend them
to the back.

beige   orange
white

futomaki (thick roll) wire
①②} 45cm for each

twist and bend them to the back.

pink green white
dark brown

black
yellow

twist and bend them to the back.

twist and bend them
to the back.

black

Japanese omelet

ume-onigiri
method of making ume-onigiri
is same as that
of nori-onigiri.

red
white
cream

onigiri(rice ball)
nori-onigiri   wire ①② 50cm△ for each twist and bend them to the back.

white black
pink

ingredients
white twist twice
brown
green

takuan(Japanese pickled radish)
make 2 pieces.
twist and bend them
to the back.
wire 20cm (for 1 piece)
twist and bend them to the back.

leaf
twist and bend them
to the back.

noodles
bowl light purple gray
wire
90cm
for each

twist and bend them to the back. (refer to page 27A)

twist and bend them to the back.

noodle
▶ 270 wind equally

chopsticks
red   pink
wire 20cm 19
(for 1 stick)
twist and bend them to the back. (refer to page 27A)

Materials

kitchen scale: small round beads/red, white, black
· wire#34/silver 260cm(104")

kitchen knife: small round beads/gray, red · wire
#31/silver 60cm(24")

scissors: small round beads/gray · large round
beads/red · wire#31/silver 60cm(24")

frying pan: small round beads/navy blue, red
· wire#31/silver 80cm(32")

apron: small round beads/light blue, yellow green
· wire#31/silver 140cm(56")

pot holder(for one.<>different color, use
the same color of beads unless otherwise indicated)
:small round beads/green<pink>, white<yellow>
· wire#34/silver 190cm(76")

▲=beginning   △=ending

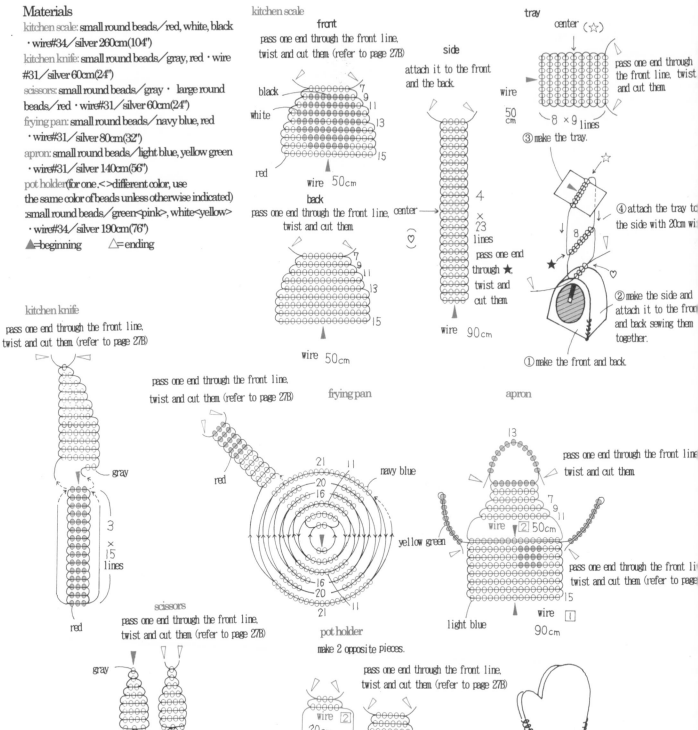

kitchen scale

front
pass one end through the front line,
twist and cut them (refer to page 27B)

black
white
red
wire 50cm

back
pass one end through the front line,
twist and cut them
wire 50cm

7
9
11
13
15

side
attach it to the front
and the back.

center
4
×
23
lines
pass one end
through ★,
twist and
cut them

wire 90cm

tray
center (☆)
pass one end through
the front line, twist
and cut them
8 × 9 lines
③ make the tray.

④ attach the tray to
the side with 20cm wire

8

② make the side and
attach it to the front
and back sewing them
together.

① make the front and back.

kitchen knife
pass one end through the front line,
twist and cut them (refer to page 27B)

gray

3
×
15
lines

red

pass one end through the front line,
twist and cut them (refer to page 27B)

frying pan

red
21 11
20
16

navy blue
yellow green

16
20
21 11

scissors
pass one end through the front line,
twist and cut them (refer to page 27B)

gray

large round beads
red

16

when you finish, twist them several times.

apron

13
pass one end through the front line,
twist and cut them

7
9
11
wire ②2 50cm

pass one end through the front line,
twist and cut them (refer to page

15
light blue
wire ①
90cm

pot holder
make 2 opposite pieces.

pass one end through the front line,
twist and cut them (refer to page 27B)

wire ②
20cm

8
9

white
<yellow>
green
<pink>
12
11
wire ① 50cm

sew 2 pieces together
with 50cm wire.

11

Then pass it through the first line,
put it together with the beginning
twist and bend them to the back.

54

pan B✱cup✱kettle✱ladle✱spatula

Materials

pan B: small round beads╱red, black・wire#31╱
silver 50cm(20″)

cup: small round beads╱white, navy blue
・wire#31╱silver 70cm(28″)

kettle: small round beads╱yellow, green・large
round beads╱green・wire#31╱silver 200cm(80″)
, wire#34╱silver 90cm(36″)

ladle: small round beads╱white, pink・wire#31╱
silver 60cm(24″)

spatula: small round beads╱white, pink・wire#31╱
silver 60cm(24″)

▲=beginning   △=ending

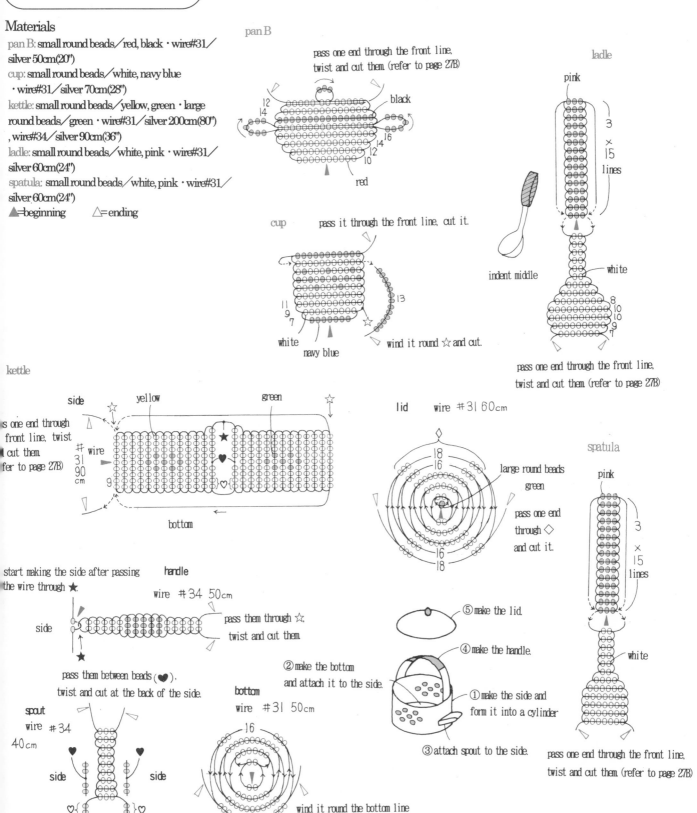

pan B

pass one end through the front line,
twist and cut them (refer to page 27B)

black

12
14

16
14
12
10

red

cup

pass it through the front line, cut it.

11
9
7

white

navy blue

wind it round ☆ and cut.

ladle

pink

3
×
15
lines

indent middle

white

8
10
10
7

pass one end through the front line,
twist and cut them (refer to page 27B)

kettle

side   yellow   green   ☆

pass one end through
front line, twist
cut them
(refer to page 27B)

wire
31
90
cm

★
♥
♡

9

bottom

start making the side after passing
the wire through ★

handle

wire #34 50cm

side

pass them through ☆,
twist and cut them.

★

pass them between beads (♥),
twist and cut at the back of the side.

spout

wire #34
40cm

♥   ♥

side   side

♡{   }♡

bottom

wire #31 50cm

16

16

wind it round the bottom line
of the side and cut.

lid   wire #31 60cm

18
16

large round beads
green

pass one end
through ◇
and cut it.

16
18

⑤make the lid.

④make the handle.

②make the bottom
and attach it to the side.

①make the side and
form it into a cylinder

③attach spout to the side.

spatula

pink

3
×
15
lines

white

pass one end through the front line,
twist and cut them (refer to page 27B)

kitchen ware

salad bowl✳measuring cup✳pan A

Materials

salad bowl(for one bowl.<>different color, use
the same color of beads unless otherwise indicated)
:small round beads／white<red>, silver<red>
・3mm bugle beads／silver<you can use any
color of beads> ・wire#31／silver 100cm(40")
measuring cup: small round beads／silver, red
・wire#31／silver 90cm(36"), wire#34／silver
90cm(36")
pan A: small round beads／light blue, yellow
・wire#31／silver 110cm(44"), wire#34／silver
110cm(44")
▲=beginning   △=ending

salad bowl

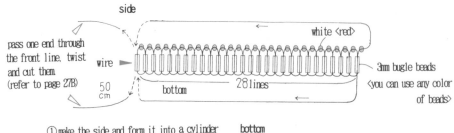

side

white <red>

pass one end through
the front line, twist
and cut them
(refer to page 27B)

wire

50
cm

bottom   28 lines

3mm bugle beads
<you can use any color
of beads>

①make the side and form it into a cylinder

bottom

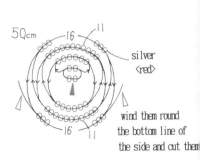

wire   50cm

silver
<red>

16   11

16   11

wind them round
the bottom line of
the side and cut them

②make the bottom and attach it to the side.

measuring cup

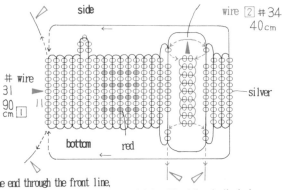

side

handle

wire ②#34
40cm

wire
31
90
cm ①

silver

bottom   red

pass one end through the front line,
twist and cut them (refer to page 27B)

twist and bend them to the back.
(refer to page 27A)

bottom

wire #34 50cm

11

wind them round the bottom line
of the side and cut them

①make the side and attach the handle to the side.

②make the bottom and attach
the handle to the side.

pan A

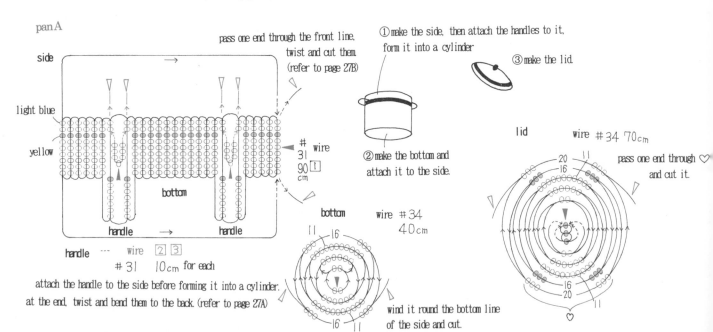

side

pass one end through the front line,
twist and cut them
(refer to page 27B)

light blue

yellow

wire
31
90 ①
cm

bottom

handle   handle

handle   ---   wire ② ③
#31 10cm for each

attach the handle to the side before forming it into a cylinder.
at the end, twist and bend them to the back. (refer to page 27A)

①make the side, then attach the handles to it,
form it into a cylinder

③make the lid.

②make the bottom and
attach it to the side.

bottom   wire #34
40cm

11   16

11   16

wind it round the bottom line
of the side and cut.

lid   wire #34 70cm

20   11
16

pass one end through ♡
and cut it.

16
20
♡

Hats · bags · shoes   hat A✳pouch✳high heels✳umbrella

Materials

hat A [pink hat]: small round beads／pink, red, yellow · wire#34／silver 120cm(48") [blue hat]:small round beads／light blue, blue, clear light blue · wire #34／silver 120cm(48") [yellow hat]:small round beads ／beige, yellow, yellow green, red · wire#34／silver 120cm(48")

pouch(for one bag including flower.<>different color, use the same color of beads unless otherwise indicated):small round beads／light blue<pink>, clear light blue<white>, green, white<red>, red <yellow> · wire#34／silver 180cm(72")

high heels(for one pair):small round beads／red, black · large round beads／black · 3mm pearl beads／gold · wire#34／gold 100cm(40")

umbrella(for one umbrella.<>different color, use the same color of beads unless otherwise indicated) :small round beads／yellow, yellow green, light blue <light blue, pink, yellow green> · wire#30／silver 20cm(8"), wire#34／silver 50cm(20")

▲=beginning   △= ending

color scheme	
pink hat	
center~6th line	pink
7th line	red
8th line	pink
9th line	yellow
blue hat	
center~6th line	light blue
7th line	blue
8th line	light blue
9th line	clear light blue
yellow hat	
center·1st line	beige
2nd line	yellow
3rd line	yellow green
4th line	yellow
5th line	beige
6th line	yellow
7th line	red
8·9th line	beige

attach the ending to 1~9 line of the opposite side.

hat A

twist and bend them to the back. (refer to page 27A)

24 20 19 18 18 13   2 3 4 5 6 7 8
1ine 1ine 1ine

9 1ines

wire 20cm center

wire 100cm

pouch

② make the carrying band with the left wire of the front.

③ make the flower (the same one as flower of the basket page 58) and attach it to the front.

wind it round the back wire and cut it.

twist and bend them to the back.

green   white <red>   red <yellow>

① make the front and the back, attach them together.

high heels

make a pair shoes with 2 line of 50cm wire.

pearl beads

twist 2~3 times.

twist and bend them to the back. (refer to page 27A)

large round beads

black   red

umbrella

llow green ght blue>

cut here

③ make the upper part of the stick.

yellow < pink>

① make this part of the stick.

② make the shade around the stick.

11

shade wire #34

stick

14 14

☆
☆

wind it round ☆ and cut it. (refer to page 27C)
leave the wire 7cm, wind it round ★ and cut it.

yellow <light blue>

yellow green <pink>

★

♥

front wire

clear light blue <white>

18 13   13 18
8

light blue <pink> center

bottom

back wire 70cm

22   22

5 line

make the pouch in the same way until 4th line, however, make the 5th line as illustrated.

this wire(30cm) is to attach the front to the back.

center

center of the front
bottom of the front
center of the back
bottom of the back attach the part in the following order.

bottom

center

wind them round ☆ and cut them.

wind them round near wire and cut them.

stick   wire #30

light blue <yellow green>

basket✳sandals✳beach sandals✳bag✳slippers✳hat B

Materials

basket(for one basket.<>different color, use the same color of beads unless otherwise indicated) :small round beads／red<yellow green>, white <yellow>, green, yellow<red> · wire#34／silver 160cm(64″)

sandals(for a pair of sandals.<>different color, use the same color of beads unless otherwise indicated) :small round beads／transparent, salmon pink<yellow green>, beige<yellow green> · wire#34／silver 200cm(80″)

beach sandals(for a pair of sandals.<>different color, use the same color of beads unless otherwise indicated):small round beads／yellow green<beige>, clear yellow<beige>, green<red>, red<white>, yellow · wire#34／silver 120cm(48″)

bag: small round beads／turquoise blue, black, gold · 4mm pearl beads／gold · wire#34／gold 90cm(36″)

slippers(for a pair.<>different color, use the same color of beads unless otherwise indicated):small round beads／white<light blue>, pink<clear light blue>, yellow<white> · wire#34／silver 160cm(64″)

hat B: small round beads／white, blue · 3mm pearl beads／gold · wire#34／silver 85cm(34″)

▲=beginning   △= ending

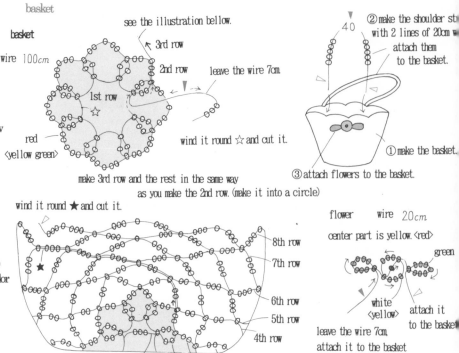

basket

basket

see the illustration bellow.

← 3rd row
2nd row
1st row
☆
leave the wire 7cm.

red <yellow green>

wind it round ☆ and cut it.

make 3rd row and the rest in the same way as you make the 2nd row. (make it into a circle)

② make the shoulder str with 2 lines of 20cm w attach them to the basket.

① make the basket.

③ attach flowers to the basket.

flower   wire 20cm

center part is yellow. <red>

green

white <yellow>

attach it to the basket

leave the wire 7cm, attach it to the basket with it.

wind it round ★ and cut it.

8th row
7th row
6th row
5th row
4th row
beginning 1st row 2nd row 3rd row

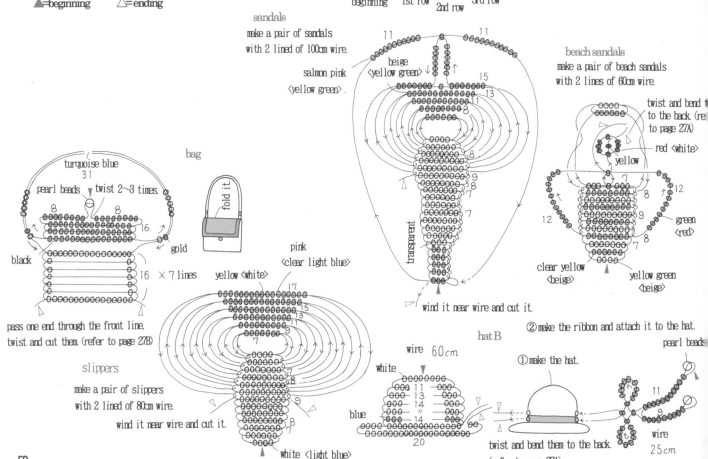

sandals

make a pair of sandals with 2 lined of 100cm wire.

salmon pink <yellow green>

beige <yellow green>

11   11

15
13
11
8

transparent

wind it near wire and cut it.

beach sandals

make a pair of beach sandals with 2 lines of 60cm wire.

twist and bend 1 to the back. (re to page 27A)

red <white>

yellow

green <red>

clear yellow <beige>

yellow green <beige>

7   12
8
7

bag

turquoise blue
31
pearl beads twist 2~3 times.

8   8

16

black

gold

16 × 7 lines

fold it

pass one end through the front line, twist and cut them (refer to page 27B)

slippers

make a pair of slippers with 2 lined of 80cm wire.

wind it near wire and cut it.

pink <clear light blue>

yellow <white>

17
15
13
11
7

7
8
9
8

white <light blue>

hat B

wire 60cm

white   11
13
14
14
blue
20

① make the hat.

② make the ribbon and attach it to the hat.

pearl beads

11
9

twist and bend them to the back. (refer to page 27A)

wire 25cm

We love an amusement park. merry-go-round✳bench✳seesaw

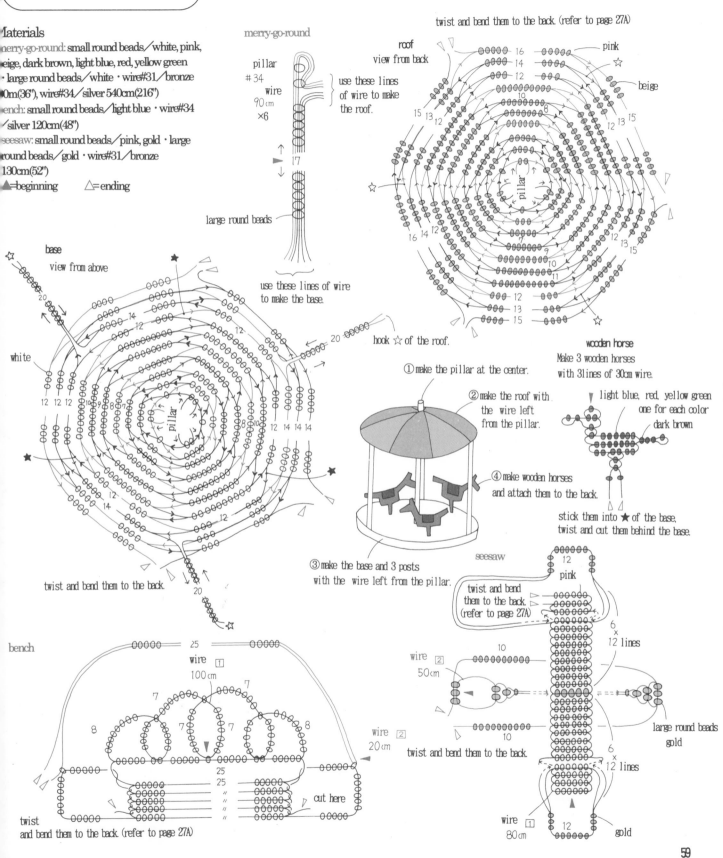

Materials
merry-go-round: small round beads／white, pink, beige, dark brown, light blue, red, yellow green・large round beads／white・wire#31／bronze 90m(36"), wire#34／silver 540cm(216")
bench: small round beads／light blue・wire#34／silver 120cm(48")
seesaw: small round beads／pink, gold・large round beads／gold・wire#31／bronze 130cm(52")

▲=beginning   △=ending

merry-go-round

pillar
#34 wire
90cm
×6

↑
↓ 17
▶

large round beads

use these lines of wire to make the roof.

use these lines of wire to make the base.

twist and bend them to the back. (refer to page 27A)

roof
view from back

pink
☆
beige

pillar

16 14 12

15 13 12

12 13 15

11
10
9
8
7

16 14 12

12 13 15

9
10
11
12
13
15

hook ☆ of the roof.

base
view from above

white

pillar

20

14

12 12 12   10 9 8 7

8 10

12 14 14 14

12

12

14

12

20

☆

twist and bend them to the back.

①make the pillar at the center.

②make the roof with the wire left from the pillar.

③make the base and 3 posts with the wire left from the pillar.

④make wooden horses and attach them to the back.

wooden horse
Make 3 wooden horses with 3 lines of 30cm wire.

light blue, red, yellow green one for each color
dark brown

stick them into ★ of the base, twist and cut them behind the base.

seesaw

12
pink

twist and bend them to the back. (refer to page 27A)

6 × 12 lines

wire ②
50cm

10

wire ②
20cm

10

large round beads gold

twist and bend them to the back.

6 × 12 lines

wire ①
80cm

12
gold

bench

25

wire ①
100cm

7   7

8   7   7   8

25
25

cut here

twist and bend them to the back. (refer to page 27A)

We love an amusement park.　　slide✳toy locomotive✳balloons✳parachute

Materials

slide: small round beads／yellow green・wire#34
／silver 220cm(88")

toy locomotive: small round beads／black, blue, red,
white・6mm hexagonal spangle／silver・wire#34
／silver 300cm(120")

balloons: small round beads／gold, light blue, red,
yellow, pink, green・wire#31／bronze 110cm(44"),
wire#34／silver 300cm(120")

parachute: small round beads／gold, pink, green,
white・3mm pearl beads／gold・wire#34／bronze
140cm(56")

▲=beginning　　△=ending

toy locomotive

slide

twist and bend them to the back.

train　make 2 trains　blue red　　spangle
for each

wire　wire □1
50cm

□2
50
cm

railroad
wire
100cm

6
×
23 lines

bottom

wire □1 100cm

wire □2
120cm

balloons

stand

①make the base,
then make the side
with the left wire.

②pass some beads through 2 sides
of the base to support the stand.

wire #31

side　gold

wire □1
50cm

bottom

wire □2
50cm

twist and bend them
to the back. (refer to
page 27A)

wire □3
10cm

bottom

8　　8

balloon
wire #34
make 5 balloons.

light blue, red, yellow, pink, green

wire □1 30cm

wire □2 30cm

string
2~3.5cm
twist

twist and bend them
to the back.

twist them to make the string

black
twist and bend them to the back.

parachute

twist and bend them to the back.
(refer to page 27A)

gold

wire □3
40cm

10

green
7

7

22

pink

white

27

7

7

7

wire □2
40cm

twist and bend them
to the back.

wire □1
60cm　Pearl beads

twist and bend them to the back. (refer
to page 27A)

We love an amusement park.) ferris wheel*tea cup

Materials

ferris wheel: small round beads／silver,
 yellow, green, orange・large round beads
／silver・wire#31／silver 890cm(356")
(or#31,770cm(308") #28,40cm(16"))
tea cup: small round beads／white, silver,
 yellow, orange, green, clear orange, blue,
 semitransparent orange, light blue・large
 round beads／white・3mm pearl beads／
 gold・wire#34／silver 220cm(88")
▲=beginning   △=ending

ferris wheel

wheel

12
↑
↓
wire
60cm
①

☆ twist and bend
them to the
back.
(refer to
page 27A)

silver

☆ = 15

with wire 2,
make in the same
way as
wire 1.

60cm

wire ③
70cm

large round beads
attach the gondola here.

twist and bend
them to the back.

gondola

make 6 gondolas.

★   ♥
00000 ■ 00000

wire ①
45cm

wire ②
45cm

each gondola to
wheel with
is large
und bead.

yellow, green, orange
make 2 gondolas for each color.
as for the disposition of gondolas,
refer to the picture on page 22.

③pick up the large round beads
which are used for attachment
of wheels, and stand
making gondola.

②tie wheels together with this wire.

①make 2 wheels.

④pass wire through the center
of the wheel and make
the base.

twist and bend them to the back.
(refer to page 27A)

base   wheel
pass them through
the center of the wheel.

9

twist and bend them
to the back.

20   20   20   20

00000 — 15 □ — 00000

↑   10   10
↑
00000 15 — 00000
wire ② 40cm

twist and bend them to the back.

use 3 lines of
40cm-wire at
a time. (or use
one 40cm-wire #28)

tea cup

twist and bend them to the back.

white

yellow

green

orange

pearl beads

semitransparent orange

light blue

blue   twist and bend
them to the back.

clear orange

11
10
8
7

silver

20

20

leave the wire 0.5cm from the end and bend it.

wire ④
40cm

wire ①
70cm

wire ②
70cm

29

large
round beads

wire ③
40cm

20

We love an amusement park. ┃ lady✴girl✴gentleman✴swing

Materials

lady: small round beads／yellow, pink, white, dark brown, ・large round beads／pink, white ・3mm curved beads／yellow, red ・5mm pearl beads／white ・wire#31／bronze 80cm(32")

girl: small round beads／red, white, dark brown ・large round beads／white ・3mm curved beads ／red ・5mm pearl beads／white ・wire#31／bronze 60cm(24")

gentleman: small round beads／yellow, white, dark brown ・large round beads／orange, white ・3mm curved beads／yellow, red ・5mm pearl beads／white ・wire#31／bronze 70cm(28")

swing: small round beads／orange, yellow, silver ・large round beads／orange, yellow ・wire#31／silver 70cm(28"), wire#34／silver 100cm(40")

▲=beginning   △= ending

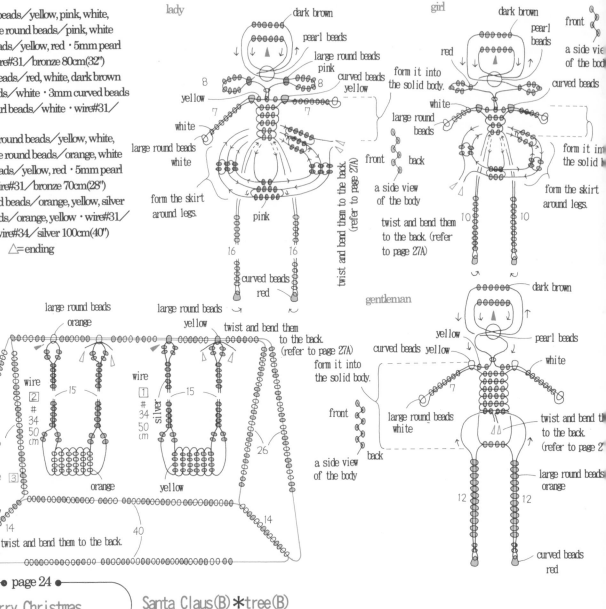

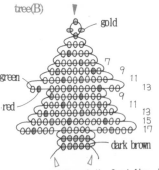

Merry Christmas ┃ Santa Claus(B)✴tree(B)

Materials

Santa Claus(B): small round beads／red, white, beige, black ・wire#31／silver 70cm(28")

tree(B): small round beads／green, gold, red, dark brown ・wire#31／silver 70cm(28")

▲=beginning   △=ending

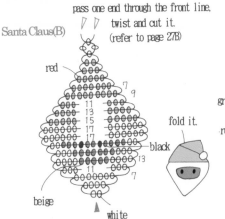

Merry Christmas

snowman ✳ socks ✳ angel ✳ Santa Claus(A) ✳ tree(A) ✳ candy cane

Materials

snowman: small round beads／white, black, red, orange・wire#34／silver 240cm(96")

socks(for one pair): small round beads／red, white, green・wire#31／silver 280cm(112") wire#34／silver 40cm(16")

angel(for one angel.<>different color, use the same color of beads unless otherwise indicated): small round beads／pink<light blue> <white>, gold・8mm doll head・wire#31／ silver 85cm(36")

Santa Claus(A): small round beads／red, white, beige, black・large round beads／white・wire #31／silver 140cm(56"), wire#34／silver 40cm (16")

tree(A): small round beads／green, gold, red, ・wire#31／silver 120cm(48")

stick(for one stick.<>different color, use the same color of beads unless otherwise indicated): small round beads／white, for long stick =pink<light blue><green>,for short stick =red<green>・wire#31／silver 30cm(12")

▲=beginning   △= ending

snowman

front put it together with the back and sew them together at the sides.

black
orange

white

wire 100cm

back wind it back to end

wire 80cm

cap wire 40cm
attach the cap to the snowman's head.

muffler
cut here   red
4 2
wire 20cm

②make the cap and attach it to the snowman's head
③make the muffler and put it around the neck.
①make the front and the back.

socks

back

white put 2 pieces together and sew them together at the sides.

wire #31. make 4 pieces using 4 wires 70cm

red

make the holly and attach it to the sock as a decoration. (refer to Yule Log page 64)

angel

wire ① 70cm
gold
doll head

put other end together with it, twist and bend them to the back. (refer to page 27A)

twist and bend them to the back.

pink <light blue> <white>

wire ② 15cm

Santa Claus(A)

front
large round beads
put it together with the back and sew them together at the sides.

black
beige   red

white
wire #31. 80cm

back wind it back to end
wire #31. 60cm

beard
make the beard attach it to the face.

pass them through ☆ bend them to the back.
white
wire #34
③make the back, put it together with the front and sew them together at the sides.

①make the front.

candy cane

long stick pink <light blue> <green>
short stick red <green>
long stick: use 40 beads.
short stick: use 30 beads.
twist and bend them to the back. (refer to page 27A)

twist and form them into the walking stick.

tree(A)

gold red green

wind it round the near wire and cut it.

63

Merry Christmas

bell✳wreath✳star✳Yule Log✳candle

Materials

bell (for one bell. <> different color, use the same color of beads unless otherwise indicated): small round beads／gold<silver> red・wire#31／silver 120cm(48")、wire#34／silver 110cm(44")

wreath (for one wreath. <> different color, use the same color of beads unless otherwise indicated): small round beads／yellow green <green>, red・wire#31／gold 110cm(44")

star: small round beads／yellow・wire#34／gold 120cm(48")

Yule Log: small round beads／brown, beige, green, red・wire#31／silver 110cm (44")、wire#34／silver 130cm(52")

candle: small round beads／white, silver, orange, green, red・wire#31／silver 120cm (48")、wire#34／silver 40cm(16')

▲=beginning △=ending

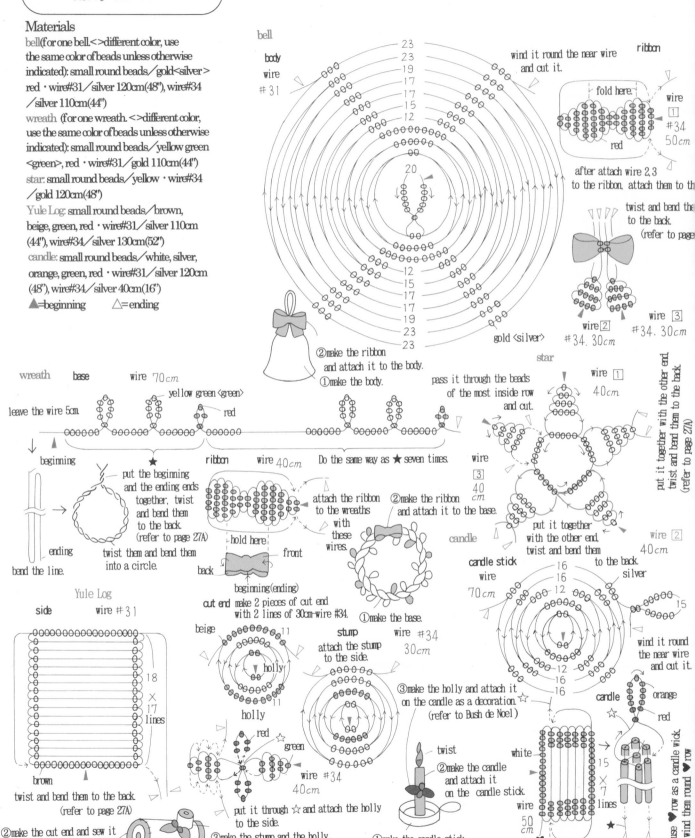

bell

body
wire #31

23
23
19
17
17
15
12

20

12
15
17
17
19
23
23

②make the ribbon and attach it to the body.
①make the body.

gold <silver>

ribbon

wind it round the near wire and cut it.

fold here
wire ① #34 50cm
red

after attach wire 2,3 to the ribbon, attach them to the

twist and bend the to the back.
(refer to page

wire ② #34.30cm
wire ③ #34.30cm

wreath base   wire 70cm

leave the wire 5cm

yellow green <green>
red

beginning

ending

bend the line.

put the beginning and the ending ends together, twist and bend them to the back. (refer to page 27A)
twist them and bend them into a circle.

★ ribbon   wire 40cm

hold here
back
front
beginning(ending)

cut end. make 2 pieces of cut end with 2 lines of 30cm-wire #34.

Do the same way as ★ seven times.

attach the ribbon to the wreaths with these wires.

②make the ribbon and attach it to the base.

①make the base.

star

pass it through the beads of the most inside row and cut.

wire ① 40cm

wire ③ 40cm

put it together with the other end twist and bend them to the back (refer to page 27A)

put it together with the other end. twist and bend them to the back.

wire ② 40cm

candle

candle stick
wire 70cm

16
16
12

12
16
16

silver

15

wind it round the near wire and cut it.

Yule Log

side   wire #31

18
×
17
lines

brown

twist and bend them to the back. (refer to page 27A)

②make the cut end and sew it together with the side.

beige
11

holly
11

holly
red ☆
green

put it through ☆ and attach the holly to the side.

③make the stump and the holly, attach them to the side.
①make the side and form it into a cylinder

stump   wire #34 30cm

attach the stump to the side.

③make the holly and attach it on the candle as a decoration ☆
(refer to Bush de Noel)

wire #34 40cm

twist

②make the candle and attach it on the candle stick.

①make the candle stick.

candle
orange
red

white

15
×
7
lines

wire 50cm

★

use ♥ row as a candle wick, wind them round ♥ row

attach it to the candle st